Grammar
in practice 4

40 units of
self-study
grammar
exercises

Roger Gower

with tests

D0318783

H45 739 078 2

CAMBRIDGE
UNIVERSITY PRESS

CAMBRIDGE UNIVERSITY PRESS
Cambridge, New York, Melbourne, Madrid, Cape Town, Singapore,
São Paulo, Delhi

Cambridge University Press
The Edinburgh Building, Cambridge CB2 8RU, UK

www.cambridge.org
Information on this title: www.cambridge.org/9780521540421

First published 2005
3rd printing 2008

Printed in Dubai by Oriental Press

A catalogue record for this publication is available from the British Library

ISBN 978-0-521-54042-1 paperback

Contents

1 So do I

Similarities

Positive:		auxiliary + *too*	Negative:		auxiliary + *either*
She **can** swim.	He **can** (swim)	**too**.	She **didn't** come.	He **didn't**	**either**.
I **like** reading.	She **does**		I **haven't** finished.	She **hasn't**	

Positive:	*So* + auxiliary + subject			Negative:	*Neither* + auxiliary + subject		
I'm cold.		**am**	I.	**I can't** cook.		**can**	I.
He'll be late.	**So**	**will**	she.	**He hasn't** got time.	**Neither**	**has**	she.
I like sport.		**do**	I.	**I don't** want lunch.		**do**	I.
She plays golf.		**does**	he.	**He doesn't** work.		**does**	she.

Differences

'I can't see.'	'**I** can!'	'I like walking.'	'**We** don't!'
'She's rich.'	'**He** isn't!'	'They'd like to be famous.'	'**I** wouldn't!'

A **Complete the statements below. Talk about similarities or differences.**

WORK QUESTIONNAIRE

	DANA	AHMED	BORJA
❶ Can you relax at work?	✓	✗	✓
❷ Do you get upset easily?	✗	✗	✓
❸ Are you enthusiastic about your job?	✗	✓	✗
❹ Do you work better in the mornings?	✗	✓	✓
❺ Are you tired at the end of the day?	✗	✗	✗
❻ Do you look forward to your holidays?	✓	✓	✓

1 'Dana can relax at work.'   'Borja __can too__ but Ahmed __can't__.'

2 'Ahmed doesn't get upset easily.' 'Dana __doesn't either__ but Borja __does__.'

3 'Dana isn't very enthusiastic about her job.'   'Borja _____ but Ahmed _____.'

4 'Borja works better in the mornings.'   'Ahmed _____ but Dana _____.'

5 'Ahmed isn't tired at the end of the day.'   'Dana and Borja _____.'

6 'Dana looks forward to her holidays.'   'Ahmed and Borja _____.'

B Match the comments by two managers about these applicants for a job.

Surname: Yoshida
First name: Shoji
Date of birth: 1981
Education: BA
(2nd class) (Politics)
Liverpool
Career: 2003–now
Political journalist (part-time)
Interests: Music, skiing and sailing

Surname: Ertl
First name: Judith
Date of birth: 1980
Education: BA
(1st class) (Politics)
Liverpool
Career history: 2002–now
Government researcher (part-time)
Interests: Skiing, yoga and music

General manager:

1 'Shoji was a student at Liverpool University.'
2 'He studied politics.'
3 'He didn't do an MA.'
4 'He's interested in music.'
5 'He's never worked in marketing.'
6 'He doesn't work full-time.'
7 'He started work in 2003.'

Personnel manager:

a 'So is Judith.'
b 'Neither does she.'
c 'So was Judith.'
d 'Neither did she.'
e 'Neither has she.'
f 'She didn't.'
g 'So did she.'

C Complete the other person's comments. For similarities, use *so* and *neither*.

1 'Shoji likes skiing.'   ' *So does Judith!* '
2 'He hasn't got a first class degree.'   ' *She has.* '
3 'She hasn't got much experience.'   ' '
4 'He isn't very old.'   ' '
5 'She's worked since 2002.'   ' '
6 'He likes sailing.'   ' '

D Write true responses for you. Use *so* or *neither*.

1 I went to university.   *So did I. / I didn't!*
2 I didn't study journalism.
3 I can ski.
4 I'm interested in politics.
5 I work full-time.
6 I've never been sailing.
7 One day I'll be a company manager.

2 He wants to stay

Verb			+ -ing form
He can't stand (= dislikes) missed		'll carry on	work**ing** in an office.
Other verbs: avoid, dislike, give up			

Verb			+ to-infinitive
I 've arranged	'll agree	can't afford	**to play** golf tomorrow.
Other verbs: 'd like, learn, manage, refuse, offer			

Verb			+ bare infinitive (−to)
They made	let		us **get up** late.

Many verbs + *to* refer to possible events in the future: expect, hope, offer, promise, want

They made us get … (= forced us to) They let us get … (= allowed us to)

A Complete the sentences with these verbs in the correct form.

> arrive   pay   stay   go   take   ~~fly~~

1 I've arranged ___*to fly*___ Singapore Airlines.

2 I'd like _____ in plenty of time.

3 Some people can't stand _____ in big, international hotels.

4 Last night I wanted to rest, but they made me _____ out to dinner.

5 Have they agreed _____ for the cost of the trip?

6 I've given up _____ my laptop on business trips.

B Write the verbs in this email in the correct form.

I managed (1) ___*to see*___ (see) the bank before I left and they agreed
(2) _____ (help) us. Fortunately, they've let us (3) _____
(continue) the existing arrangements about the money we owe them and offered
(4) _____ (lend) us an extra million dollars for a new factory.
Unfortunately, they have refused (5) _____ (give) us any more than a
million dollars and they're going to make us (6) _____ (pay) it back
over five years. I've given up (7) _____ (ask) the other banks for
money so we can only afford (8) _____ (build) one new factory.

C Use a verb and continue these sentences for you.

1 I can't stand *doing housework./waiting for buses.*

2 I've given up _____

3 I miss _____

4 I've learnt _____

5 I would like to carry on _____

3 I know. It's raining

Present simple or present continuous?   ▶▶ Verb forms page 67

We use the present simple	We use the present continuous
• for things that are always true:	• for things happening now:
I **come** from Australia.	Look! It**'s** rain**ing**.
• for situations that stay the same for a long time:	• for a temporary situation around now:
She **lives** in France.	She**'s** study**ing** economics.
• when we say how often something happens:	• for changing situations:
She **always sleeps** late.	It**'s** gett**ing** dark.
Do you **often get up** early?	
I don't **usually have** breakfast.	
I **clean** my teeth **every day**.	

Non-action verbs like *feel, know, love, (not) matter, need, prefer, see, think, understand, want* are not usually used in the continuous.

Adverbs like *always, never, rarely, sometimes, usually* go before the main verb and after *'m/is/are/was/were:* He's always nice.
Longer expressions like *every day, once a week* usually go at the end of a sentence.

A Underline the correct alternative in these extracts from a letter.

1 We **always go**/We go always to our local art gallery when there's an exhibition on.

2 Nikita **sing/sings** in a choir and **usually has/is usually having** rehearsals once or twice a week.

3 I **like/'m liking** the ballet but Nikita **prefers/is preferring** the opera.

4 **We sometimes go/We're sometimes going** to the opera and sometimes the ballet.

5 Do you and your wife **like/likes** opera?

6 We both **read/are reading** a lot so **once or twice a week we go/we once or twice a week go** to the library to borrow some books.

7 At the moment I **read/'m reading** *Palace Walk* by Naguib Mahfouz. **Does you/Do you** know it?

B Write the questions in the present simple or present continuous and then answer about you.

1 (you/often/go) *Do you often go* to the opera?   *No, I don't.*

2 How often (you/go) _____ to rock concerts? _____

3 (like/you) _____ rap music? _____

4 (you/sometimes/listen to) _____ jazz? _____

5 (you/read) _____ a good book at the moment? _____

6 (you/prefer) _____ the cinema or the theatre? _____

C Write the verbs in these postcards in the present simple or present continuous.

1

The sun _is shining_ (shine) and I _____ (sit) by the pool and _____ (relax) before the 10,000 metres race tonight. I _____ (not/like) missing my usual routine of a light jog in the afternoon but it's much too hot to train.

2

I _____ (feel) I _____ (get) lazy. I _____ (not/train) this week and I _____ (need) to lose a bit of weight. At the moment I _____ (eat) about 7,000 calories a day, twice as much as a normal man! That's OK before a competition, because then I _____ (need) to keep up my weight, but not when I'm on holiday!

3

I _____ (spend) the day in bed today because I _____ (have) a bit of a headache. It _____ (not/matter), though, because it _____ (rain) very hard outside and we can't play. They _____ (always/play) this competition on grass.

4

I _____ (write) this in Central Park. I _____ (wait) for my friend and it _____ (get) a bit cold. We _____ (always/run) together for at least an hour and then we _____ (do) some weight training in the gym. After that, the real hard work begins! All this week I _____ (practise) at 80% speed both on my back and my front.

D Match the postcards in C with these professional sportspeople.

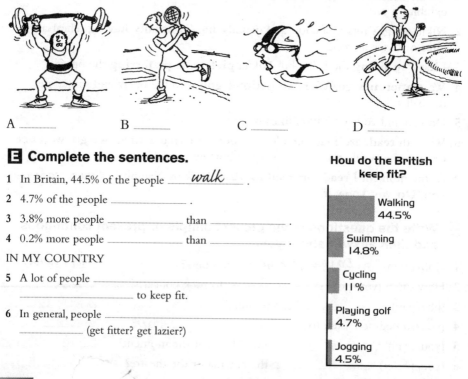

A _____   B _____   C _____   D _____

E Complete the sentences.

How do the British keep fit?

1 In Britain, 44.5% of the people _walk_ .

2 4.7% of the people _____ .

3 3.8% more people _____ than _____ .

4 0.2% more people _____ than _____ .

IN MY COUNTRY

5 A lot of people _____ _____ to keep fit.

6 In general, people _____ _____ (get fitter? get lazier?)

Walking 44.5%

Swimming 14.8%

Cycling 11%

Playing golf 4.7%

Jogging 4.5%

4 My birthday's in August

A Write *at, on, in* or *X* (nothing) in the gaps.

1 _in_ the evening 2 _____ the 20th century 3 _____ 4.30 am
4 _____ Saturday 5 _____ the evening 6 _____ my birthday 7 _____ midnight
8 _____ last year 9 _____ the summer holiday 10 _____ Tuesday morning
11 _____ night 12 _____ tomorrow 13 _____ an hour 14 _____ dinner time

B Look at the project diary and complete the sentences below.

PROJECT DIARY: NEW LUXURY CAR

YEAR 1
Feb: budget
20 March: first meeting (project team)
April: design ideas
1 May: best idea
Summer/Autumn: first designs

YEAR 2
Last week of Jan: engineers – first model
12.00 1 December: first model → directors
YEAR 3
Spring – road tests
Tuesday 1 September: cars → public!

1 _In February_ the directors worked on the budget.
2 _On 20 March_ there was the first meeting of the project team.
3 _____ we discussed design ideas and _____ the directors decided on the best idea.
4 _____ and _____ we prepared the first designs.
5 _____ the engineers started work on the first model.
6 _____ we showed the first model to the directors.
7 _____ the drivers road tested the car.
8 _____ the company started to sell the new car to the public.

5 She'll be able to help

can/could (for general ability)

I **can/can't** swim. (in the present)
I **could/couldn't** swim when I was six. (in the past)

ⓘ *can* has no infinitive or past participle. So we use *able to*
- for the future: I'**ll be able to** speak Danish soon. I'm having lessons.
- for the present perfect: I'**ve never been able to** drive.
- for the *-ing* form: I enjoy **being able to** play the piano. I'm glad I had lessons.
- for the infinitive: I'd like **to be able to** afford a new car.

managed to/was able to/couldn't (for a single event/specific achievement in the past)

I **managed to** (**was able to**) get some tickets for the match last night. (positive)
I **couldn't** (**wasn't able to**) get any tickets for the match last night. (negative)

ⓘ *managed to* and *couldn't* are more informal than *was able to* and *wasn't able to*.
We use *managed to* when we succeeded in doing something difficult.

A Underline the correct alternative.

It's amazing. Only a few years ago most people (1) **can't/<u>couldn't</u>**
even use a computer. Now they use the most incredible
technology every day of their lives. If they want to send videos
to each other, they (2) **can/could** send them by mobile phone
and soon they (3) **can/'ll be able to** buy a mobile phone
which plays all their music. And, for several years now, thanks to
the internet, people (4) **can/have been able to** work from
home. Many parents like (5) **can/being able to** spend more time
with their children and many would love to (6) **can/be able to**
give up going to the office completely. There's no problem with
the technology. Even now, we (7) **can/could** get all the
information we need online and we (8) **can/was able to**
communicate with anyone we want to at the press of a button.

B Complete the sentences with the correct form of *can, could, be able to* or *manage to*.

1 Did you ..... *manage to* ..... fix the TV?

2 Unfortunately, I .... afford to buy a washing machine until last year.

3 Some of the instructions are too complicated. I .... understand them.

4 If we get up early, we'll probably .... buy a hi-fi system in the
sales.

5 She tried five times to send the email. Finally, she .... send it.

6 The hair-dryer's broken. I haven't .... use it for two days.

7 Ask Jade about using the remote control. She'll .... help you.

6 Neither of them play tennis

both (= A + B)			+ positive verb	
Both	children/the children/my children/Tom and Sara			
Both of	them/the children/my children		go	to school.
They **both**				

ⓘ We can also say with positive verbs: They are **both** hard workers. I know them **both**.

neither (= not A and not B)			+ positive verb	
Neither (child)			likes languages. (singular)	
Neither	my son	**nor**	my daughter	speaks/speak Portuguese.
Neither of	them/the children/my children			
Neither	my son **nor** my **daughters**		speak Portuguese. (plural)	

ⓘ A plural verb is more informal after *neither ... nor* + singular noun and *neither of*.

either (= A or B)
Sara **(either)** does her homework in the library **or** (in) the computer room. (positive)
Sara likes **(either)** biology **or** geology – I can't remember which.
Tom doesn't like **(either)** maths **or** physics. (negative)
Does **either child** swim? Does/Do **either of them**/**either of the children** swim?
ⓘ A plural verb is more informal after *either of*.

A Underline the correct alternative in the sentences below.

SEASHORE CAMP
Small site by the sea
Shops in nearby village
Large restaurant
Children's play area
No pets!

SUN CAMP
* Small family campsite 200 metres from the sea
* Nearest shop 1 km
* Small coffee bar
* Play area for children
* Sorry – pets not allowed.

1 <u>**Both**</u>/**Neither** campsites are near the sea.

2 **Either/Neither** of them have a shop on the site.

3 There's no nightclub – **either/neither** at Seashore Camp or Sun Camp.

4 **Either/Neither** campsite allows pets.

5 They're **both/either/neither** good campsites.

6 'Does **either/neither** the Seashore Camp or the Sun Camp have a play area for children?' 'Yes, **both/either** of them do.'

7 'Do **both/either/neither** of them have a swimming pool?' 'No, **both/either/ neither** of them does.'

B Complete this email with *both*, *either* or *neither*.

I've stayed at (1) ___*both*___ sites and I like them (2) _____ .
(3) _____ of them are very large, but there'll be no problem getting in –
(4) _____ one or the other will have spaces available. (5) _____ of
them have a lovely family atmosphere and children are obviously welcome,
but (6) _____ allow pets so unfortunately you won't be able to bring your
dog. At the Seashore, you can eat well, (7) _____ at lunchtime or in the
evening, but the Sun Camp only has a small coffee bar. (8) _____ the
Seashore nor the Sun Camp are very lively at night – there isn't a nightclub
at (9) _____ site – but (10) _____ the owners are lovely people and
they make you feel at home.

C Complete the second
sentence so that it
means the same as
the first. Use *both*,
neither or *either*.

1 Ben is in his teens and Sarah is too.
  Both Ben and Sarah are in their teens.
2 Uncle Harry didn't get married until he was 40 and Uncle Bill didn't either.
  _____ until they were 40.
3 Granny doesn't like Aunt Pat and she also doesn't like Aunt Mary.
  _____ Aunt Mary.
4 Kate was married before and so was Max.
  _____ married before.
5 Ken is an accountant or a lawyer – I can't remember which.
  _____ a lawyer – I can't remember which.
6 Dad enjoyed the wedding and Mum did too.
  _____ enjoyed the wedding.
7 Nick couldn't come and Claudia couldn't either.
  _____ could come.

7 He called to say goodbye

Infinitive of purpose (to say why we do something)		
Verb	+ *to*-infinitive	OR + *for* + noun
I'm going to the library	to borrow a book.	for a book.
She turned on the TV	to watch the news.	for the news.
You need more money	to buy a car.	for a car.
I need more time	to finish the report.	for the report.

ⓘ In more formal contexts we can say *in order to*:
The government put up taxes in order to pay for better health care.

A Use the words in brackets to answer the questions.

Wedding
29 May
Simon ~ Nicki

1 Why are you working so hard? (earn lots of money)   *To earn lots of money.*
2 What do you need the money for? (my wedding)   *For my wedding.*
3 Why are you going to the bank? (cash a cheque)   ....
4 Why are you phoning the florists? (order some flowers)   ....
5 What are you going to the jeweller's for? (a ring)   ....
6 Why are you going into town? (hire a suit)   ....
7 What are you meeting your brother for? (some advice!)   ....

B What did Simon do? Complete the sentences. Use the phrases from the list and verbs from the box.

| check |
| ~~take~~ |
| send out |
| meet |
| hire |
| prepare |

TO DO
- ~~book a photographer~~
- employ a chef
- phone a car rental company
- go to the post office
- drive to the airport
- phone the bank

1 He   *booked a photographer to take*   some photographs.
2 He   ....   the food.
3 He   ....   the wedding transport.
4 He   ....   the invitations.
5 He   ....   the bride's parents.
6 He   ....   his bank balance!

8 Did they?

Reply questions

	Auxiliary verb + pronoun		
'I've got four brothers.'	'Have	you?	That's a lot!'
'Anna was born in Prague.'	'Was	she?	I didn't know she was Czech.'
'They can't speak Russian.'	'Can't	they?	I thought they lived in Russia!'

We use 'reply questions' (*Have you? Was she? Can't they?*) to show interest or surprise.

For present/past simple sentences add *do or does/did*:
'I walk to work.' 'Do you? Why? Haven't you got a car?'
'She doesn't eat meat.' 'Oh, no. Doesn't she? Does she eat fish?'
'We got married last year.' 'Did you? I didn't know that.'

A Fill the gaps with reply questions from the box.

AMAZING
FACTS

> Did it?   Do they?   ~~Are there?~~   Was it?   Did he?
> Are they?   Isn't it?

1 'There are only 12 letters in the Hawaiian alphabet.' '*Are there?* I didn't know that.'

2 'Languages are dying at a rate of more than one a month.' '................
That's terrible.'

3 'More people speak English in China than in the USA.' '................
How amazing!'

4 'French was the official language of England for 300 years.' '................ Are you sure?'

5 '*Canada* came from the native American word for *big village*.' '................
That's interesting!'

6 'Basque is not related to any other language in the world.' '................ Why's that?'

7 'Shakespeare invented the word *assassination*.' '................ I never knew that!'

B Write reply questions and add a sentence like the sentences in A.

DID YOU KNOW ...?

1 A rat can live longer without water than a camel.   *Can it? That's amazing.*

2 Jaguars are scared of dogs.   ....

3 A giraffe sleeps for only 1.9 hours a day.   ....

4 Whale oil was used in some cars until 1973.   ....

5 Alligators can't move backwards.   ....

6 The pelecanimimus, a bird-like dinosaur, had over 220 teeth!   ....

7 More people are killed by donkeys than die in air crashes.   ....

8 Some frogs can be completely frozen and then come back to life.   ....

9 I was working when she arrived

Past continuous	Past simple ▸▸ Verb forms page 67
At 10.00 pm I was driving home.	At 10.15 pm I had an accident.

We use the past continuous for long temporary actions, or situations not complete at a time in the past.
We use the past simple for short completed actions.

when

I was driving home **when** I had an accident. I had an accident **when** I was driving home.
When I was driving home, I had an accident.
Compare:
When I came home, the phone was ringing. (The phone was ringing before I came home.)
When I came home, the phone rang. (I came home and after that the phone rang.)

while/as

While/As I was driving home, I had an accident. (NOT I was driving ... as/while I had ...)
John was watching TV. (Two long actions at the same time.)
When we talk about two past actions that continued for the same period of time we can often use the past simple after *while/as*: **While/As** I drove home, John was watching TV.

ⓘ We do not usually use the past continuous for 'state' verbs like: *want, like, be.*

A Write the verb in the correct form and match the sentences with the pictures. Who are the people?

A _____ B _____ C _____ D *David and Victoria Beckham* E _____

1 They first (meet) ___*met*___ while he (relax) ___*was relaxing*___ at a party after a football match. ___*D*___

2 She (fall) _____ in love with him while she (work) _____ as a newspaper reporter. _____

3 He (speak) _____ to her while she (have) _____ lunch at the singer Sting's house. _____

4 He first (kiss) _____ her when he (go) _____ to a party at her father's house. _____

5 She first (see) _____ him as he (climb) _____ a ladder at an exhibition of her art. _____

B Write the verbs in the correct places in the past simple or past continuous.

1 *work/discover*   In 1928 Sir Alexander Fleming ___*discovered*___ pencillin by accident while ___*he was working*___ in his laboratory.

2 *look/notice/enjoy*   In 1995, at exactly the same time, two men _____ through their telescopes, when they _____ a new comet in the sky. Alan Hale was in New Mexico and Tom Bopp _____ a 'star party' with some friends in Arizona. The comet is now called the Hale-Bopp comet.

3 *sit/start/work out/fall*   In 1667 Sir Isaac Newton _____ under an apple tree when an apple _____ to the ground. He _____ to think about the movement of the apple and _____ the scientific reason why objects fall to the ground.

4 *turn into/realise/cook/work on*   In 1946 Dr Percy LeBaron Spencer _____ an experiment with radio waves when a peanut bar in his pocket _____ liquid. He then _____ that short electric waves _____ food very quickly. The first microwave oven was sold in 1954!

5 *need/sing/think/come to*   In 1974 Art Fry _____ of the idea of Post-Its in his local church. The idea _____ him while he _____ in the choir and he _____ a bookmark for the songs in his choir book.

6 *dig/turn out/find*   In 1709 a land worker _____ some pieces of a statue as he _____ a well near the volcano Vesuvius. It _____ to be part of the lost city of Herculaneum.

C Write one sentence, using *when*, *while* or *as*. Put the verbs in the past simple or past continuous.

OUR BOAT ADVENTURE IN MEXICO

1 Last year my brother and I (fish). We (make) an amazing discovery. WHEN
   Last year my brother and I were fishing when we made an amazing discovery.

2 At 3.00 pm my brother (sleep) in his cabin. I (sunbathe).   WHILE

3 I (stand up). I (notice) part of an old boat under the water.   AS

4 I (wait) for my brother to wake up. I (jump) into the water.   WHILE

5 I (swim) around the boat. I (see) a beautiful Mayan statue.   AS

10 I must go

must/have to

I **must** go to the doctor's. I don't feel very well. (I feel it's necessary.)

I **have to** go the doctor's. She wants to see me. (Another person makes it necessary. It's not my opinion.)

You **mustn't** use a mobile phone on a plane. (It's necessary **not** to use a mobile phone. Don't!)

You **don't have to** get up early today. Stay in bed. It's Sunday. (It's not necessary.)

When we use the past or the *will* future, we use *have to*:

I **had to** go to the doctor's yesterday. I'll **have to** go to the dentist's soon.

ⓘ We can use *must* when we want to suggest or recommend something strongly:

You **must** listen to this CD – it's great. (Please listen. I feel it's necessary.)

A Underline the correct alternative in these sentences.

1 I **must/mustn't** remember to be polite. I'm talking to a human, not a computer.

2 Many people **must/have to** pay to go online, so I **must/mustn't** send unnecessary emails!

3 I **mustn't/don't have to** use emoticons, but they can be great fun when writing to friends.

4 If I email a company, I'**ll must/'ll have to** be more formal.

5 I **must/have to** remember to check my spelling.

6 I **mustn't/don't have to** write all the words in capital letters. They look like I'm shouting.

B Write the correct form of *must* or *have to* in the sentences. What's the job – nurse, flight attendant, police officer? _____

1 When I'm on duty I _____*have to*_____ wear a uniform. I look very smart in it. I _____ send you a photo sometime! (By the way, you _____ send me one of you and your new baby!)

2 Unfortunately, we _____ work very long hours, and three nights last week I _____ get up in the middle of the night and go to work.

3 Luckily, we _____ use computers – I hate computers!

4 Of course, we _____ smoke when we're on duty.

5 You _____ be formal with people but you should always be polite and smile. You _____ lose your temper!

6 Before I started, I _____ have a medical examination.

7 I _____ work in a very narrow space, which isn't always easy.

8 When we get to a country, we sometimes _____ work for several hours, so we can relax and go sightseeing.

Test 1 (Units 1–10)

A Circle the correct alternative.

1 'I didn't like that film.' **So do I./So did I./Neither do I./Neither did I.**

2 She's given up **to smoke/smoking**.

3 You're very quiet. What **do you think about/are you thinking about**?

4 We always finish work early **in/on/at** Fridays.

5 Soon you **can/'ll be able to** drive really well.

6 I don't know who's on the phone. It's **both/either** your mother or your sister.

7 He got up early **to do/doing** his exercises.

8 'I don't eat meat?' **'Do you?/Don't you?** I never knew that.'

9 We stayed at the party because we **were enjoying/enjoyed** ourselves.

10 You **must/have to** phone me soon and tell me all the news!

10

B Complete the sentences with *so/neither/either/both*.

1 'I've been to Taiwan once.' '_____ have I.'

2 'She can't play chess.' 'He can't _____.'

3 _____ films were very exciting. We enjoyed them enormously.

4 Your two friends were very rude. I didn't like _____ of them.

5 _____ his brother nor his sister play the guitar.

5

C Write the verbs in the correct form.

1 Why don't you offer _____ (help) her?

2 Please let me _____ (come) with you.

3 You can't carry on _____ (spend) so much money.

4 When are you leaving home _____ (go) to university?

5 I miss not _____ (have) a room of my own.

5

D Complete the sentences with one of the verbs in the correct form.

1 Can you speak up? I _____ hear you. (can/not, not/manage)

2 She _____ work since she fell ill two months ago. (can/not, not/able to)

3 It was difficult but we _____ get there on time. (could, manage to)

4 He _____ go home early today. He wasn't very well. (must, have to)

5 Don't worry! This letter isn't important. You _____ reply. (not/have to, must/not)

5

E Complete the sentences with *at, on, in* or *X* (nothing).

1 They arranged to meet us _____ 6.00 am _____ the morning.

2 She was born _____ 1989 _____ September 2nd.

3 I'll see you _____ lunchtime _____ Friday.

4 You can get here _____ ten minutes.

5 Where were you _____ Wednesday evening _____ last week?

5

F Write the verbs in the correct form of the present simple/continuous or past simple/continuous.

1 These days he _____ (come/usually) to work in jeans.

2 Look over there! Who _____ (she/talk) to?

3 I really _____ (not/understand) this exercise. Can you help me?

4 He _____ (shave) when he _____ (hear) the news.

5 When I _____ (see) him yesterday, he _____ (talk) to his manager.

6 It suddenly _____ (begin) to rain last night as I _____ (walk) home.

6

G Write the correct reply question (e.g. *Can't they?*).

1 'I love travelling by plane.' '_____ I don't!'

2 'She earns more than he does.' '_____ Where does she work?'

3 'We didn't like the concert.' '_____ Why not?'

4 'I wasn't very well last night.' '_____ What did you have to eat?'

4

H Correct the mistakes.

1 'I feel tired this morning.' '<u>So I do</u>. Let's go back home.' _____

2 Why did you <u>make me to get up</u> so early? _____

3 We <u>are rarely seeing</u> each other these days. _____

4 What is she doing <u>at the tomorrow</u>? _____

5 After three hours we <u>could</u> find something to eat. _____

6 <u>Neither my brothers</u> are married. _____

7 I sat down <u>for to rest</u>. _____

8 'She's had a difficult life.' '<u>Did she</u>? Why?' _____

9 He broke his arm while he <u>skied</u>. _____

10 You <u>don't have to</u> cross the road here. Stop! _____

10

TOTAL **50**

11 However, he was very tired

Linking words

We use *although/even though* (= contrast) and *as/since* (= *because*) to link parts of a sentence:
Although/Even though he was ill, he went to work. (He was ill. He went to work.)
He went to work **although/even though** he was ill.
As/Since the weather was fine, we had a picnic. (The weather was fine. We had a picnic.)
We had a picnic **as/since** the weather was fine.

We use *however* (= contrast) and *too, as well, also, what's more* (= more information) to link ideas across sentences:
I'd love to come to dinner on Friday. **However**, I'm busy that night. / I am, **however**, busy that night / I'm busy that night, **however**.
Alberto lives in England. Anna lives in England, **too**. / Anna lives in England **as well**. / Anna **also** lives in England.
It's an interesting job. **What's more**, it's well paid.

ⓘ Note from the examples above the position of the words in the sentence and when we use a comma. (EXAMPLE: However, …)

A Underline the correct alternative in these encyclopedia extracts.

1 People say jazz started in New Orleans in the 1890s. <u>However,</u>/Although there were probably other places in the American south with similar music.

2 There are African influences in jazz. There are **also/too** European influences.

3 Street bands were important **since/even though** musicians first learnt to play their instruments in them.

4 However,/Although there were many great early musicians, Louis Armstrong was by far the most important.

5 In the 1920s, jazz became popular throughout the USA. **What's more,/Too,/ As well**, it influenced other types of music.

B Use a linking word/phrase to complete these extracts from a biography of Louis Armstrong.

1 _____As/Since_____ Louis' family was very poor, he had to earn money by singing on street corners.
2 In the 1920s he played trumpet in the great Kid Ory band. He _____ played for King Oliver.
3 His technique on the trumpet was extraordinary. The sound was beautiful, _____ .
4 _____ Louis was well known in Europe, he didn't tour there until the mid 1930s.
5 He had a happy personality. _____, the Civil Rights situation for blacks made him angry.
6 _____ he enjoyed playing so much, he continued performing in public until his death in 1971.

20

12 Could I open the window?

Permission		
Can I (informal) Could I (polite) Could I possibly (very polite) May I (formal)	borrow some money?	Yes, you can. /No, you can't.
Giving/refusing permission: You **can/can't** borrow my computer.		

Requests	
Can you (informal) Could you please (polite)	help me?
Would you mind (very polite)	helping me?

A Complete the sentences.

1 Pets welcome | Can I _bring_ my dog? | _Yes_, you _can_.

2 **No Parking** | Could I _____ here? | _____ you _____.

3 Could I possibly _____ my friend. | Sorry, _____, you _____.

4 AMERICAN EXPRESS | May I _____ by credit card? | _____, you _____.

5 Room free | You _____ use this room if you like.

6 Keep off the grass | Sorry, you _____ walk on the grass.

B Complete the requests with imperatives from the box in the correct form.

> Wait a minute. Shut the door. ~~Tell me the time.~~ Bring me the bill.
> Lend me a pen. Look after the children.

1 Could you please _tell me the time_? I haven't got a watch.
2 Would you mind _____? I've left mine at home.
3 Can you _____? It's freezing in here.
4 Could you please _____? There's no hurry.
5 Would you mind _____? They're too young to be on their own.
6 That was delicious! Now can you _____? My taxi's waiting.

13 She's gone

Present perfect or past simple?

▶▶ Verb forms pages 67–68

We use the **present perfect** when we think about the past and the present together
* to talk about a past action that affects the present:
  Oh, no! **I've left** the tickets at home. I can't get into the theatre.
  The President **has arrived** in Britain. He is having talks with the Prime Minister.
* for general experiences in the past:
  She's really interesting. She**'s been** all over the world and **(has) met** many famous people.
* to talk about an unfinished time period:
  I've lived in this town for five years, and I still live here.
  I've been on three business trips this year.

We use the **past simple** when we think only about the past
* for completed actions/states/habits at a specific time in the past:
  I **went** to Madrid last Thursday. I **lived** in Moscow ten years ago.
  I **met** her **yesterday**. (NOT ~~I've met her yesterday.~~)
* to give details of news of recent events:
  The President has arrived in Britain. His plane **landed** at 10 o'clock.

ⓘ He**'s gone** to Tibet. (= He's there now.)
  He**'s been** to Tibet. (= He went but now he is back.)

A Underline the correct answers in these extracts from an article about the actress Nicole Kidman.

1 She <u>was</u>/have been born in Hawaii but she <u>grew up</u>/
  's grown up in Sydney.

2 She **always had/has always had** an extraordinary
  enthusiasm for her work.

3 She first **appeared/has appeared** on stage when she **was/
  has been** five and she **was/has been** an actress ever since.

4 When she was 18, she **appeared/has appeared** on TV for the first time.

5 She **made/has made** her first US film *Dead Calm* in 1989.

6 She likes the actor Russell Crowe and they **were always/have always been**
  very good friends. Last year they **spent/has spent** a week together in Fiji.

B Complete these extracts from an interview with Nicole Kidman. Use the correct form of the present perfect or past simple.

1 '(you/ever/acted) *Have you ever acted* on television?' 'Yes, I *have*.'
  ' When (be) _____ that?' '(I/appear) _____ in
  a series called *Vietnam* when I was 18.'

2 '(you/ever/win) _____ an Oscar?' 'Yes, I _____.'
  'What part (you/play) _____?' 'I (be) _____ the writer, Virginia
  Woolf, in *The Hours*.'

3 '(you/accept) _____ the part immediately?' 'No, I _____. At first I (not/want) _____ it but friends (persuade) _____ me.'

4 '(you/ever/go) _____ to the Cannes Film Festival?' 'Of course!' 'When (you/last/go) _____?' 'I (go) _____ last year, to tell people about *Dogville*.'

5 '(you/ever/feel) _____ like giving up acting?' 'Not really, I (always/be) _____ very committed to my work.'

C Complete the sentences. Use the present perfect and past simple once in each answer.

1 Guess what? I/meet/a wonderful man. We/go/to the cinema together last night.

Guess what? *I've met a wonderful man. We went* to the cinema together last night.

2 Bad news! Tara/just/give up/her job. Apparently, she/not like/her boss.

Bad news! _____ her boss.

3 It's all right. I/just/find/my wallet. It/be/in my old jacket.

It's all right. _____ my old jacket.

4 I've just heard. Sam/have/an accident. His car/hit/a tree.

I've just heard. _____ a tree.

5 Oh, no! We/miss/the match. It/start/at 5.00.

Oh, no! _____ at 5.00.

D Write the verbs in the present perfect or past simple.

CLOSE FRIENDS

1 **The rock musician Brian Eno and the painter and composer Tom Phillips**

BRIAN: I *first met* (first/meet) Tom at Art School and he _____ (be) one of my tutors. I _____ (always/admire) him because he's a serious artist.

TOM: I _____ (know) Brian for 40 years. At Art School, he _____ (look) quite strange, even though he _____ (dress) conservatively. Brian _____ (be) a very bright student, and after he _____ (leave) college, he _____ (start) to keep in touch. Over the years, he _____ (always/give) me great support.

2 **The punk singers Siouxsie Sioux and Marc Almond**

SIOUXSIE: I _____ (first/see) Marc in a leather shop in London and I _____ (tell) him I really liked his music. We _____ (get on) well immediately. In recent years Marc _____ (change) a lot and _____ (become) more confident. We're still great friends.

MARC: Siouxsie and I _____ (now/reach) a similar stage in our careers and we can choose our projects. When Siouxsie _____ (move) to France a few years ago, we _____ (see) each other less often. The last time we _____ (meet) was at a party in Paris.

14 Do you know when he left?

Direct	Indirect		
	Question phrase		Subject + verb
How old is Bob?		how old	Bob is?
Where does Sue work?	Do you know	where	Sue works?
When do the shops open?	Can/Could I ask you	when	the shops open?
What have they done?	Can/Could you tell me	what	they have done?
When will she come?	Would you mind telling me	when	she will come?
Who is he meeting?		who	he is meeting?

Indirect questions sound less confident and are more polite/formal than direct questions.
We sometimes use indirect questions when we want to 'distance' ourselves from the question
because we are not confident, or the question is unusual and possibly rude:
Would you mind telling me what your salary is?

ⓘ We do not use *do/does/did* in the second part of indirect questions.

A Write the questions in a more polite way.

1 How often do you visit our city?
Could you tell me *how often you visit our city* ?

2 Where do you usually stay?
Could I ask you _____ ?

3 When was your last visit?
Would you mind telling me _____ ?

4 How long are you staying this time?
Can I ask you _____ ?

5 How did you get here?
Would you mind telling me _____ ?

6 Which areas have you visited?
Can you tell me _____ ?

7 What improvements would you like to see?
Do you know _____ ?

B You're in a new city. Use the words to write polite questions.

1 where/(be)/the post office? *Do you know where the post office is?*
2 what time/(close)/the bank? _____
3 which floor/(be)/the café on? _____
4 where/(can/I/leave)/my bags? _____
5 when/(leave)/the train? _____
6 how much/(cost)/the ticket? _____

15 He lives by the sea

under	above	below	by	against	inside	outside

 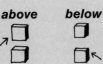

We use *on* for
- surfaces: **on** the table/his finger/page 40
- a position on a river, lake, sea, road: the town is **on** the river/the way/the road/the coast
- floors of a building: **on** the first floor

We use *in* to show a position inside a larger place: **in** a box/hospital/the taxi/a book/Brazil

We use *at* to show
- places/group activities where people do things and where things happen: He was waiting **at** the corner/the bus stop/my house/work/the doctor's. He's studying **at** school/university. I'm enjoying myself **at** a party/a concert.
- a place on a journey: This plane stops **at** Brussels. Wait **at** the end of the road.

ⓘ We use *inside* (instead of *in*) to emphasise the inner part of something: Let's stay **inside** the car – it's too cold outside.

A Underline the correct preposition.

1 I'll meet you <u>outside</u>/**above** the church **against/under** the bridge.

2 Leave your bike **above/against** the wall.

3 My flat is **against/by** the river.

4 There are three floors. I don't live **in/on** the top floor. I live on the floor **above/below**.

5 The people in the flat **above/below** me, on the top floor, make a lot of noise.

6 When we get **inside/under** the flat you'll have to shout!

B Complete this text with the correct preposition.

STRATFORD-UPON-AVON

Stratford-upon-Avon is one of the prettiest towns (1) _*in*_ (in/on/at) England. It is (2) _____ (in/on/at) the beautiful county of Warwickshire (3) _____ (in/on/at) the River Avon and is famous because of William Shakespeare. Shakespeare was born there (4) _____ (on/at) a house in Henley Street, (5) _____ (in/on) the centre of the town, and went to school (6) _____ (at/on/by) the local grammar school, which was built in 1428. One mile from Stratford, (7) _____ (in/on) the small village of Shottery, you'll find the family home of Anne Hathaway, Shakespeare's wife. The Hathaways lived (8) _____ (in/on/by) the house from 1470 until the late 19th century. It is believed that it was (9) _____ (in/on) this house, (10) _____ (in/on/by) the fire, that Shakespeare asked Anne to marry him.

16 What time does the film start?

Predictions: *will* or *going to*?

We use *will*/*'ll* when we expect something to happen, based on our experience/knowledge:
They**'ll** be here by six. (I'm sure.) They **won't** be late. (They never are.)

We use *going to* when there is something in the present which will make something happen in the future:
I feel ill. (present) I think I**'m going to** be sick. (future)
Be careful! (present) You**'re going to** fall. (future)

Future events: present continuous or present simple?

We use the present continuous (+ a time expression) for definite personal arrangements:
Andy**'s coming** to see me **later this evening**. I**'m going** away **tomorrow**.
We use the present simple (+ a time expression) for public timetables and programmes:
The bus **leaves in half an hour**. My English classes **finish next week**.

A Complete the predictions. Which is more likely – *will* or *going to*?

1 The waiter's carrying too many plates. He __*'s going to*__ drop them.

2 Rock 'n' roll _____ disappear by June. (*Variety* newspaper, in 1955)

3 No woman _____ be Prime Minister in my lifetime. (Margaret Thatcher, in 1974)

4 Look at my son! He's growing very quickly. He _____ be very tall.

5 Man (not) _____ fly for fifty years. (The first man to fly a plane, Wilbur Wright, in 1901)

6 People _____ soon get tired of television. (The movie producer, Darryl Zanuck, in 1946)

7 Look out! He _____ faint.

8 Man (never) _____ reach the moon. (The inventor, Dr Lee de Forest, in 1967)

B Jon is talking about a business trip. Write sentences using the present simple or present continuous.

1 I/meet/Annika/in Stockholm/tomorrow *I'm meeting Annika in Stockholm tomorrow.*

2 The plane for Sweden/leave/at 6.30 am _____

3 It/get/in/to Arlanda airport/at 10.10 _____

4 We/have/lunch/at the Sturehof _____

5 We/meet/her manager/after lunch _____

6 We/go/to the Södra theatre/in the evening _____

7 The play/start/at 7.30 _____

8 It/finish/at about 11.00 _____

17 Do you know if she's there?

Direct	Indirect (more polite/formal)		
	Question phrase		Subject + verb
Have they left? Did he buy a car? Can she speak English? Do they live here? Is it going to rain?	Do you know Can/Could you tell me Have you any idea Would you mind telling me	if/whether	they've left? he bought a car? she can speak English? they live here? it's going to rain?

In indirect *yes/no* questions *if* and *whether* mean the same.

A Complete the questions. Write the words in the correct order.

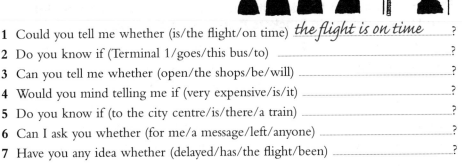

1 Could you tell me whether (is/the flight/on time) *the flight is on time* ?
2 Do you know if (Terminal 1/goes/this bus/to) _____ ?
3 Can you tell me whether (open/the shops/be/will) _____ ?
4 Would you mind telling me if (very expensive/is/it) _____ ?
5 Do you know if (to the city centre/is/there/a train) _____ ?
6 Can I ask you whether (for me/a message/left/anyone) _____ ?
7 Have you any idea whether (delayed/has/the flight/been) _____ ?

B Write the questions you ask at a company in a more polite way.

1 Are there any written instructions for this product?
   Could you tell me *whether there are any written instructions for this product* ?
2 Do you buy it directly from Sony?
   Can I ask you _____ ?
3 Have you ordered from them before?
   Would you mind telling me _____ ?
4 Are they working with any other company like yours?
   Do you know _____ ?
5 Will you order from them next year?
   Have you any idea _____ ?
6 Did you come to our annual conference?
   Can I ask you _____ ?
7 Are you going to continue with the research?
   Can you tell me _____ ?

18 A computer is a machine which ...

Defining relative clauses

We use a relative pronoun to add information about a noun.
We use *who/that* (for people) and *that/which* (for things/animals):
The man **who** buys old furniture isn't here. (**The man** isn't here. **He** buys old furniture.)
That's the medicine **which** is good for colds. (That's **the medicine. It** is good for colds.)

Sometimes the relative pronoun is the **subject** of the relative clause:
I have a cat **that** sleeps all day. This is the camera **which** doesn't work.

Sometimes the relative pronoun is the **object** of the relative clause:
I have a cat **that** I feed twice a day. This is the camera **which** he bought yesterday.

ⓘ We often leave out the relative pronoun when it is the object:
I have a cat (which) I feed twice a day.

A Join the parts of the definitions, using a relative pronoun. Put the relative pronoun in brackets if you can leave it out.

1 vegetarian: someone _who_
2 glue: something ....
3 bee: a yellow insect ....
4 scissors: something ....
5 champion: a person ....
6 lawyer: someone ....

a people use to stick things together
b makes honey
c wins a competition
d we use to deal with a legal situation
e doesn't eat meat or fish
f people use to cut hair or paper with

B Complete the definitions. If possible, leave out the relative pronoun.

1 An optician is someone (test/people's eyes) _who/that tests people's eyes._
2 A surgeon is a doctor (do/medical operations) ....
3 A bandage is a piece of cloth (we/tie round/an injury) ....
4 A thermometer is something (measure/our temperature) ....
5 An antibiotic is a medicine (we take/to cure infection) ....
6 A dentist is someone (we see/when we've got toothache) ....

C Join the sentences with *who*, *which* or *that*. If possible, leave out the relative pronoun.

1 I saw the doctor. She was very nice. → The _doctor I saw was very nice._
2 She's the doctor. She looked after me. → She's ....
3 She gave me antibiotics. They were very strong. → The ....
4 I went to the hospital. It is near where I live. → The ....
5 I had an operation. It was a great success. → I ....
6 The nurses looked after me. They were great. → The ....

28

19 I'm learning English so that ...

so (that) + modal (can/could, will/would) (= purpose)

I stayed at work	**so (that)**	I	could	finish the report.
I've drawn a map		you	won't	get lost.

ⓘ Another way of saying the same thing is with an infinitive of purpose:
I stayed at work **to finish** the report. (= My purpose/aim was to finish the report.)

so ... + adjective/adverb (that) (= result)

He was	**so**	tired	**(that)**	he went to bed.
We arrived		late		we almost missed the party.

ⓘ so + adjective + (that) makes the adjective stronger. Compare:
He was so tired (that) he went to bed. (= He was very tired. The result was he went to bed.)
He was tired, so he went to bed. (NOT ... ~~so that he went to bed.~~)

A Join the sentences with *so (that)* and
write extracts from the magazine article.
Use the modal in brackets.

LIVING THE DREAM?

1 'I gave up my job. I wanted to spend more time with my family.' (could)
   He *gave up his job so (that) he could spend more time with his family.*

2 'We moved to the country. We wanted the children to have a better way of life.'
   (would) They ⎯⎯⎯⎯⎯⎯⎯

3 'We sold our flat in the city. We hoped to have enough money to buy a farm.'
   (would) They ⎯⎯⎯⎯⎯⎯⎯

4 'We lived near a small village. We wanted to get to know people more easily.'
   (could) They ⎯⎯⎯⎯⎯⎯⎯

5 'We grew our own vegetables. We didn't want to have to buy them.'
   (would) They ⎯⎯⎯⎯⎯⎯⎯

B Choose adjectives to make sentences with *so (adjective) (that)*.

hard	poor	small	~~busy~~	happy	expensive

1 We were ⎯⎯ *so busy (that)* ⎯⎯ we didn't have time to talk to each other.

2 The farms were ⎯⎯⎯⎯⎯⎯⎯ we couldn't afford one.

3 Our house was ⎯⎯⎯⎯⎯⎯⎯ there was no room to move.

4 At first, we were ⎯⎯⎯⎯⎯⎯⎯ we couldn't afford to buy anything.

5 Life was ⎯⎯⎯⎯⎯⎯⎯ we got depressed.

6 But after a year, we were ⎯⎯⎯⎯⎯⎯⎯ we decided we could never go back!

20 The film was amazing

Adjectives ending in -ing/Adjectives ending in -ed

Adjectives ending in -ed normally say how people feel:
I'm very excit**ed** about the trip. I'm very relax**ed** when I'm on holiday.
Adjectives ending in -ing normally describe the people or things that cause the feelings:
The trip will be very excit**ing**. My holidays are always very relax**ing**.

amazed	amazing	depressed	depressing	interested	interesting
amused	amusing	exhausted	exhausting	irritated	irritating
annoyed	annoying	fascinated	fascinating	satisfied	satisfying
bored	boring	frightened	frightening	surprised	surprising
confused	confusing	horrified	horrifying	worried	worrying

A Underline the correct adjective in these sentences.

1 'I liked *Die Another Day* but I was a bit **annoyed**/annoying by some
of the special effects.' 'Oh, I thought the whole film was **bored/boring**.'

2 'Was the Brazilian film *City of God* **depressed/depressing**?' 'Not at all.
It was **fascinated/fascinating** and the acting was **amazed/amazing**.'

3 'I was **horrified/horrifying** by *Red Dragon*.' 'Oh, I wasn't. I thought
Anthony Hopkins was very **amused/amusing**.'

4 'I was **amazed/amazing** by Wang Xiaoshuai's *Beijing Bicycle*. It was very dramatic.'
'Yes, I agree. And I thought the characters were very **interested/interesting**.'

5 'Some people were **irritated/irritating** by Almodóvar's last film.' 'Not me. I was
fascinated/fascinating by the story. But then, I like all Almodóvar's films.'

B Complete the text with adjectives in the correct form.

When I first read the *Star Wars* novels, I was (1) _surprised_ (surprise) how well-written they
were. They're really (2) .... (excite), although I got (3) .... (bore) with
them after a while. I thought *Star by Star* was quite (4) .... (amaze), and easily the
most (5) .... (satisfy) of the novels, but I was a bit (6) .... (irritate) by
Dark Journey. The characters were (7) .... (fascinate) but I got (8) ....
(confuse) by the plot, and the ending was rather (9) .... (disappoint). Parts of the
novel were still (10) .... (interest), though.

C Underline the correct alternative for you and complete the sentences.

1 **I'm**/I'm not very _interested_ in art. (interest)

2 **I think/don't think** English grammar is .... (confuse)

3 **I'm/I'm not** .... when I travel by air. (frighten)

4 **I'm sometimes/I'm never** .... by films or books. (shock)

5 **I think/I don't think** the political situation in my country is
.... (worry)

Test 2 (Units 11–20)

A Circle the correct alternative.

1 **Although/However** it was raining, we went for a walk.

2 Sorry. You **can't/couldn't** leave now. Please wait.

3 I've **been/went** to Disneyland when I was a child.

4 Could you tell me where **do you live/you live**?

5 He was hiding **under/above** the table.

6 I **stay/'m staying** at home this evening.

7 Have you any idea if **she is/is she** at home?

8 He took the bag **who/which** was on the table.

9 It was **so dark that/dark so that** I couldn't see a thing.

10 What a **fascinating/fascinated** idea!

10

B Complete the sentences with words from the box.

> As   even though   also   However   too

1 The weather wasn't very good. ...., the picnic was a great success.

2 .... you're never in when I phone, I'll send you an email.

3 He sings beautifully. He can dance well, ...

4 I'm going to buy a new car .... I haven't got much money.

5 I like walking. I .... like cycling.

5

C Use the words in brackets to complete the sentences.

1 Can I ask you what time (you/want/to leave tomorrow) ....?

2 Would you mind (answer/the phone) ....?

3 Could I (use/your computer) ....?

4 Do you know what (be/the time) ....?

5 Could you tell me whether (he/like/French food) ....?

5

D Complete the sentences with at, in, on, outside or against.

1 I've got the money. It's .... my pocket.

2 I put my bike .... the wall. It won't fall over.

3 My wife's still .... work. She won't be home before 7.00 pm.

4 The restaurant is .... the second floor.

5 I live in a small apartment just .... London.

5

E Write the verbs in the correct form.

1 _____ (go) to Germany before? (present perfect or past simple)

2 She looks very upset. I think she _____ (cry). (*will* or *going to*)

3 I _____ (just/hear) the news. Congratulations! (present perfect or past simple)

4 Look at the timetable. The boat _____ (leave) at 10.30 pm. (present simple or *will*)

5 When _____ (you/arrive) in New York? (present perfect or past simple)

5

F Join the sentences with *who, which* or *that*. If possible, leave out the relative pronoun.

1 This is the woman. She lives next door. This _____

2 That's the man. I was telling you about him. That's _____

3 He bought a coat. He didn't really like it. He _____

4 I stayed in a hotel. It had a swimming pool. The hotel _____

5 The boy spoke English. He showed us the way. The boy _____

5

G Use the words in brackets to complete the sentences.

1 He stood up so _____ a better view. (could get)

2 He stood up to _____ a better view. (get)

3 I was so _____ two pizzas. (hungry/eat)

4 I was hungry so _____ two pizzas. (eat)

5 They spent a year in Japan so _____ Japanese. (could learn)

5

H Make an adjective and complete the sentences.

1 Sorry. I'm completely _____ . Tell me again. (confuse)

2 I had a very _____ dream last night. (frighten)

3 The train's going to be an hour late. How _____! (annoy)

4 What are you so _____ about? (worry)

5 It's been a very _____ day. (exhaust)

5

I Correct the mistakes.

1 May I <u>to pay</u> by cheque? _____

2 I<u>'ve seen</u> her three years ago. _____

3 Could you tell me <u>what time does the plane leave?</u> _____

4 That's the woman <u>who I met her</u> at the party. _____

5 He was feeling ill, <u>so that</u> he went to the doctor's. _____

5

TOTAL

50

21 She's really nice

Gradable adjectives	Ungradable adjectives (= extreme adjectives)	
cold angry difficult interested tired good/nice	freezing furious impossible fascinated exhausted brilliant	
Adverb of degree (to make the adjective stronger)	**+ gradable adjective**	
very awfully terribly incredibly really	cold angry difficult interesting tired good/nice	
Adverb of degree (to emphasise the adjective)	**+ ungradable adjective**	
really absolutely	freezing furious impossible fascinating exhausted brilliant	
completely totally	impossible exhausted	

We normally emphasise ungradable adjectives when we want to sound dramatic.
Note that different adverbs are used with different adjectives.

A Complete the sentences with an ungradable adjective from above.

1 'You look awfully tired.' 'Yes I'm absolutely ......*exhausted*......'

2 'Why are you angry?' 'Angry? I'm absolutely .... The neighbours kept me awake.'

3 'It's terribly cold.' 'It looks absolutely .... Where's my big coat?'

4 'It'll be difficult to find a taxi today.' 'It'll be totally .... How will I get there?'

5 'Ask Tim to take you.' 'That's an absolutely .... idea! Thanks.'

B Choose one of the adjectives and an adverb of degree to complete the sentences about a hiking adventure.

1 When I started, the weather was ......*really nice*...... (nice/fascinated).

2 It was .... (cold/exhausted) but the sun was shining.

3 I got lost and was .... (difficult/furious) with myself.

4 It was .... (angry/impossible) to turn back now.

5 When night came it was .... (tired/freezing) and I was .... (good/tired).

6 The rescue team was .... (good) and gave me hot coffee!

C Choose an adjective and write true sentences about you.

1 I (angry/furious) ..*was (incredibly) angry/(absolutely) furious when I lost my watch.*..

2 I (tired/exhausted) ....

3 I (interested/fascinated) ....

4 .... was .... (difficult/impossible)

5 .... was .... (good/nice/brilliant)

22 It was so hot

so + adjective/adverb			such (+ a/an) (+ adjective) + noun		
She's		generous.	She's		a generous person.
The weather was	so	hot.	It was	such	hot weather.
These shoes look		comfortable.	They look		comfortable shoes.
It was **so** cold	(that)	we stayed at home.			
It was **such** a cold day					

We use *so/such* to emphasise what we're saying.

ⓘ There are **so many** people. / There are **such a lot of** people.

A Write the words in the correct order.

1 country such a is beautiful Taiwan
   Taiwan is such a beautiful country.

2 varied culture so is the

TAIWAN

3 wonderful eaten food such we've ....

4 day had a lovely we such ....

5 so holiday quickly has our gone ....

B Write so or such in these guidebook extracts.

1 The National Palace Museum is *so* interesting that visitors spend several days there.

2 Shin-Lin Night Market is .... a lively place you'll want to stay until 3 am.

3 Taroko Gorge is .... beautiful that it will stay in your memory forever.

4 Lion's Head Mountain has .... many temples.

5 Taiwan has .... a lot of wildlife that six national parks have been set up.

C Join the sentences with so or such.

1 It was a very nice day. We walked round the city.
   It *was such a nice day (that) we walked round the city.*

2 It is a very big city. We soon got tired.
   The city ....

3 We were very hungry. We stopped at the Hsing Yeh restaurant for a meal.
   We were ....

4 The dishes were very large. We couldn't eat everything.
   They ....

5 It was a lovely meal. We left a big tip.
   The meal ....

34

23 She's a friend of his

We use possessive adjectives + noun
- to say something belongs to someone: They're **my** photos. That's **her** car.
- to talk about relationships: Have you seen **their** father? Where are **his** parents?
- before parts of the body and clothes: He put **his** hands in **his** pockets.

We use possessive pronouns without a noun
- to say something belongs to someone: Those photos are **mine**. That car's **hers**.
- after articles and *this/that/these/those*: He's **a** friend of **mine**. Where are **those** shoes of **his**?

We use a noun with *'s* (and *s'* for plural) + noun
- for people: Tom**'s** job, a boys**'** school, men**'s** names, Jan**'s** mother**'s** car; for animals: the cat**'s** ears; for time expressions: last week**'s** concert, in two weeks**'** time

We normally use *of*
- when something is a part of a thing/place: the side **of** the house, the top **of** the hill
- with people when there is a long phrase: the address **of** one of the people I met

We use noun + noun in everyday combinations: a **bus station**, the **front-door key**

A Underline the correct alternative in these sentences.

1 He closed **the/<u>his</u>** eyes and sang.

2 It's **Andrea's guitar/the guitar of Andrea**.

3 It's **my/mine** cello. It's been **my/mine** for ages.

4 Those old records of **our/ours** are very valuable.

5 Is this **Tom's parents'/Tom's parent's** piano?

6 Have you seen **my violin case/the case of my violin**?

7 I loved the opera. The **womens'/women's** costumes were very beautiful.

8 She was getting ready for **tomorrow's concert/the concert of tomorrow**.

9 He lost **the/his** voice in the middle of the concert.

10 What's **the song name/the name of the song**?

B Join the nouns to make extracts from a news report. Change the order of the nouns if necessary.

Classical Music Awards

1 Andrea Bocelli has one of the (world/most exciting voices) *world's most exciting voices* .

2 (Sir Simon Rattle/recording) _____ of (opera/Beethoven) _____ won a prize.

3 (The name/the mezzo-soprano, Cecilia Bartoli,) _____ _____ is known throughout the world.

4 (guitar/Alexandre) _____ makes a beautiful sound.

5 (The results/this year/competition) _____ were announced at (the concert/the end) _____ .

35

24 She's much older than I am

London is **wetter/more expensive than** Rome. (more)
London has got a **bigger population than** Rome. (more)

My job is **as good/tiring as** yours. (the same)

Tim is**n't as intelligent/friendly as** his brother. (less)

ⓘ For some longer adjectives we can use *less … than*: Tom is **less friendly than** his brother.

To express a big difference:
London is **much/far/a lot** wetter than Rome. London has got a **much/far/a lot** bigger population than Cambridge. Tom isn't **nearly as** friendly **as** his brother.

To express a small difference:
London is **a bit/a little** more expensive than Rome.
My job is **nearly/is almost/isn't quite as** good as yours.

A Choose an adjective from above and compare the people. Use a comparative + *than*, or *(not) as … as*.

	Eddie	Frank	Bill
Born	15.6.80	7.7.80	21.12.71
Height	1.76 m	1.98 m	2.2 m
Weight	92 kg	79 kg	79 kg

1 Eddie and Bill (young) *Eddie is younger than Bill.*
2 Eddie and Bill (tall) *Eddie isn't as tall as Bill.*
3 Bill and Eddie (heavy) ....
4 Bill and Frank (light) ....
5 Frank and Eddie (almost/old) ....
6 Bill and Frank (nearly/young) ....
7 Eddie and Bill (much/short) ....
8 Frank and Eddie (a bit/tall) ....

B Complete the witness's sentences.

1 He was *much younger than* .... (much/young) this man.
2 He wasn't .... (quite/good-looking) the man over there.
3 That man is .... (far/suntanned) the thief.
4 The thief wasn't .... (nearly/thin) this man.
5 He had .... (a lot/big) nose than this man.
6 I think he was .... (a little/tall).

25 I look forward to seeing you

Adjective	+ preposition	+ -ing form
He was **afraid**	**of**	los**ing** his job.
Also: good/bad/brilliant **at**; worried/pleased/excited **about**; tired **of**; interested **in**; keen **on**		

Noun	+ preposition	+ -ing form
Have you got any **ideas**	**for**	improv**ing** sales?
Also: the advantages **of**; the trouble **with**; a delay **in**		

Verb	+ preposition	+ -ing form
I **insist**	**on**	see**ing** the doctor.
Also: think **of**; succeed **in**; look forward **to**; feel **about**		

A Complete these advertisements with the correct preposition and the verb in the correct form.

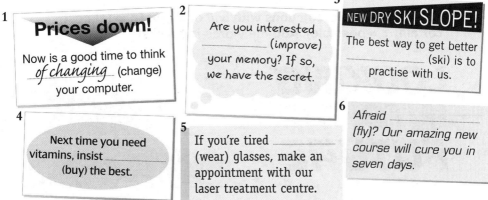

1

Prices down!

Now is a good time to think _of changing_ (change) your computer.

2

Are you interested .... (improve) your memory? If so, we have the secret.

3

NEW DRY SKI SLOPE!

The best way to get better .... (ski) is to practise with us.

4

Next time you need vitamins, insist .... (buy) the best.

5

If you're tired .... (wear) glasses, make an appointment with our laser treatment centre.

6

Afraid .... (fly)? Our amazing new course will cure you in seven days.

B Complete this memo with a preposition and the correct verb.

MEMO

To: RT (Sales)

From: HJ (Product Development)

The Managing Director is worried (1) _about losing_ (lose/find) more customers again this year. I'm keen (2) .... (finish/develop) the youth market and I have some ideas (3) .... (attract/change) younger customers into our shops. Do you know an advertising company that will be good (4) .... (create/remove) a new image for us? Of course we need to succeed (5) .... (buy/sell) our clothes products to people of all ages and I'm a little afraid (6) .... (return/upset) our older customers, so we need to have an image that will attract everyone. How do you feel (7) .... (use/think) the company that advertises our food products? They're good.
I look forward (8) .... (hear/believe) your suggestions.

26 It might rain

will (= I'm certain)

I'll see you tomorrow. I **won't** see you tomorrow.
I'll **definitely** see you./I **definitely** won't see you. (emphatic – without doubt)
I'll **probably** see you./I **probably** won't see you. (almost certain)
I'm sure/I expect/I doubt if/I don't think I'll see you tomorrow.

may/might (= it's possible but I'm not sure)

We **might/may** arrive late this evening.
We **mightn't/might not/may not** arrive late this evening. (NOT ~~mayn't~~)
I think we **might** arrive late this evening.

'Have you finished painting the kitchen?' 'No, I haven't, but I **will** later.'
'Are you going to Italy next year?' 'I **might/may**, but I haven't decided yet.'
'Will it snow later?' 'It **might/may**, but it **might/may** not.'

ⓘ *may* and *might* mean the same but *might* is more common in spoken English.

A Complete these predictions with *will* or *might* (✓ = (almost)
certain; ? = possible). Add the words in brackets.

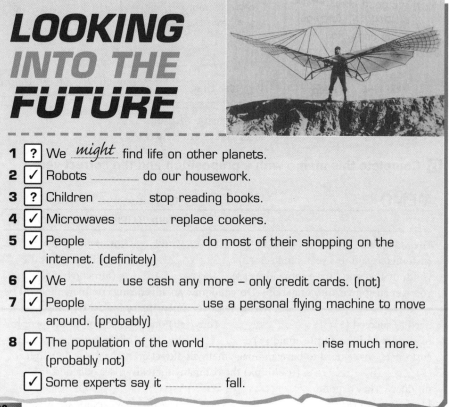

LOOKING INTO THE FUTURE

1 ? We _might_ find life on other planets.

2 ✓ Robots .... do our housework.

3 ? Children .... stop reading books.

4 ✓ Microwaves .... replace cookers.

5 ✓ People .... do most of their shopping on the
internet. (definitely)

6 ✓ We .... use cash any more – only credit cards. (not)

7 ✓ People .... use a personal flying machine to move
around. (probably)

8 ✓ The population of the world .... rise much more.
(probably not)

   ✓ Some experts say it .... fall.

B **A scientist is making predictions about global warming. Use the words to write sentences.**

1 sure/world/get warmer

    I'm sure the world will get warmer.

2 sea levels/definitely/rise

3 farmers/probably/not/be able to/plant their crops near the sea

4 not/think/some small islands/survive

5 the world's weather/definitely/get more extreme

6 expect/some parts of the world/get drier

7 other parts of the world/might/get colder

8 unfortunately,/doubt/we/ever/learn to look after our environment

C **Give your views on some of the predictions in A and B.**

1 *I don't think we will/I think we might* find life on other planets.

2 _____ stop reading books.

3 _____ do most of their shopping on the internet.

4 _____ the world's weather _____ worse.

5 _____ more storms.

6 _____ destroy the environment.

D **Complete these sentences for you with *think/be sure/expect/doubt* and *will, might/may, won't, might not*.**

1 *I think I might/I don't think I'll* get a pay rise next month.

2 _____ live to be a hundred years old.

3 _____ change my car in the next two years.

4 _____ live here all my life.

5 _____ a long holiday next year.

27 If I were you ...

We use the first conditional to talk about things that may or may not happen:

If + present (real situation)	+ will/shall, may/might, can, must (result)
If there's a good film on television,	I might watch it.
If you hear of a cheap house for sale,	you must give me a ring.

We use the second conditional to talk about unreal situations:

If + past (unreal situation)	+ would/might (result)
If I became President (but I won't),	I would build more hospitals.
If I could speak good French (but I can't),	I might live in France. (could = past of can)
If I were you (but I'm not),	I'd get a new car. (giving advice)

ⓘ We can reverse the order of clauses in most *if* sentences:
You must give me a ring if you hear of a cheap house for sale.

ⓘ We can use *were* for all persons in formal or informal English. We can use *was* after *I/he/she* but it is informal.

ⓘ The situations are 'real' or 'unreal' often because the person **thinks** they are real or unreal.

A Match the two parts of the sentences about pay discussions.

1 If you give up your company car,   a we'll stop work immediatlely.

2 It would be difficult to get to work   b we'll pay all your transport costs.

3 If we give you a 3% increase,   c we'd have to close the company.

4 The company would have no money   d if we gave up our company cars.

5 If you don't give us more money,   e if we gave you a 10% pay rise.

6 If you went on strike,   f you'll have to work longer hours.

B The managers are talking about the pay discussions. Underline the correct alternative.

1 They **might change/change** their minds if the Chief Executive **might talk/talked** to them.

2 If I **am/were** you, **I'd/I'll** offer longer holidays.

3 If we **will want/want** them to agree, you **didn't/mustn't** lose your temper.

4 I **might feel/must feel** differently if they **will be/were** more polite.

5 If we **increased/would increase** their pension, how much **does/would** it cost?

6 I **offer/'ll offer** free health insurance if you **would think/think** it's a good idea.

7 We **can/were able to** start again now if you **are/will be** ready.

8 If we **will get/get** an agreement today, **I'd buy/I'll buy** you a drink!

C Are these situations possible or 'unreal' for you?
Write conditional sentences with *will* or *would*.

1 Someone offers you a new job next week.
(possible) If someone offers me a new job next week, I'll say no. OR
(unreal) If someone offered me a new job next week, I'd say no.

2 You have toothache tomorrow.

3 You live to be eighty years old.

4 You decide to have a party next week.

5 Your computer is stolen.

6 You wake up very early tomorrow morning.

D Give advice, using *If I were you* and ideas from the box.

> learn Chinese before you go   buy a new one   ~~look for another job~~
> go by boat   put on a coat

1 'I don't earn much money.' *If I were you, I'd look for another job.*
2 'I'm cold.'
3 'I'm afraid of flying.'
4 'My car's very old.'
5 'I'm going to live in China.'

E What would you do in these situations? Write conditional
sentences with *would* (= I'm certain) or *might* (= it's possible).

1 Your company offers you a well-paid job in Canada.
If my company offered me a well-paid job in Canada, I might accept it.

2 You hear someone screaming in the house next door.

3 An attractive, wealthy person wants to marry you.

4 You meet the US President in the street.

5 You speak English fluently.

28 They hurt themselves

Subject pronouns

Singular					Plural		
I	you	he	she	it	we	you	they

Reflexive pronouns

| myself | yourself | himself | herself | itself | ourselves | yourselves | themselves |

Subject	Verb (+ preposition)	(Direct/Indirect) Object	
She	cut	herself.	
He	looked at	himself	in the mirror.
We	taught	ourselves	Arabic.

We use a reflexive pronoun when the object of a verb is the same as the subject.

We often use reflexive pronouns with these verbs:
ask behave burn buy dry enjoy get help hurt introduce look after make see talk to tell watch

We do not usually use reflexive pronouns with these verbs:
change dress feel get dressed get up meet relax shave wash

ⓘ We use *by* + reflexive pronoun to mean 'alone' or 'without help':
She went to the cinema by herself. I mended the car all by myself.

A **Underline the correct alternative in these sentences.**

1 I don't like Liz. She's always talking about **she/herself**.

2 Have you two introduced **yourself/yourselves**?

3 Just **relax/relax yourselves** and have a good time!

4 That man's amazing! He taught **he/himself** to play the guitar in just three weeks!

5 My husband sings to **him/himself** in the shower. He's got a great voice.

6 I was wearing my work clothes. I had to **change/change myself** very quickly to get here on time.

7 Are you **enjoying/enjoying yourself**, Paul?   Yes, thanks. It's a great party.

8 I bought **me/myself** a new BMW but I can't really afford it.

9 I'm sorry, I'm going home. I don't **feel/feel myself** very well.

10 Phil and Tania first **met/met themselves** at a party just like this one.

B Complete the sentences with a reflexive pronoun.

1 'Those two people seem to be enjoying _themselves_ a lot!'
2 'We're going into the kitchen to make .... a cup of coffee.'
3 'My father's very old now. He sits in his chair and talks to .... all day.'
4 'Why don't you two help .... to some food? It's very good.'
5 'What's happened to your hand? Have you hurt ....?'
6 'Yes, I cut .... on a broken glass.'
7 'I'll give you a lift home in my new car. It's an automatic. It almost drives ....!'
8 'Goodbye, Sabina. Look after ....'

C Complete the sentences with by + a reflexive pronoun.

1 My cousin doesn't like living with other people. He prefers to live _by himself_ .
2 No one ever helps my mother with the cooking. She always does it ....
3 Our cat loves climbing trees, but it can't get down .... so I have to go up and get it!
4 I usually go to the cinema with friends. I don't like going ....
5 My younger brothers are very clever. They managed to learn about computers ....

D Complete the sentences with verbs from the box and a reflexive pronoun.

| watch   ask   tell ... about   ~~pay for~~   look after   behave   buy   teach |

1 My sister's got a lot of money. When she goes on holiday, she can afford to _pay for herself_ .
2 Simon's got a job in Japan so he's .... Japanese.
3 My sister's children are very polite. They always try to .... in front of visitors.
4 We've got a very old car so this year we're going to .... a new one.
5 My grandfather lives with us. He's too old to ....
6 I sometimes ....: 'Should I leave home?'
7 My sister always comes when we show old family videos. She loves .... on TV!
8 I've done all the talking. Now .... me ....! How big is _your_ family?

29 She must be rich

	must/may/might/could/can't		
Certainty			
You	must	be	tired!
They	can't/couldn't	have	much money.
Possibility			
He	may/might/could	be	out.
He	may not/might not		

! We cannot say: ~~He mustn't have much money.~~ (certainty) ~~He can be out.~~ (possibility)
They must be tired! (= I'm sure they're tired.)
They might be out. (= It's possible they're out.)
They can't have much money. (= I'm sure that they don't have much money.)
They may/might not have much money. (= It's possible that they don't have much money.)

A Match the pairs of sentences.

1 That can't be George Clooney.　　　　a Look at all those photographers.
   That must be George Clooney.　　　　b He looks too young.

2 She can't be a famous model.　　　　a She's not attractive enough.
   She might be a famous model.　　　　b She's very attractive.

3 That can't be her husband.　　　　a He's wearing a wedding ring.
   That might be her husband.　　　　b Her husband's got grey hair.

4 That must be Sean Penn.　　　　a I recognise his smile.
   That might not be Sean Penn.　　　　b But he looks just like him.

B Look at the photos of young stars and complete the sentences opposite with the correct modal.

1 2 3
4 5 6

1 It _____can't_____ be Justin Timberlake. (must/can't) This is a girl, not a boy!

It _____might_____ be Britney Spears. (might/might not)

2 It _____ be David Beckham. He looks quite sporty. (might/mustn't)

3 It _____ be Leonardo DiCaprio. He looks just like that! (can't/must)

4 It _____ be Brad Pitt. He's got the same smile! (can't/might)

5 It _____ be Catherine Zeta-Jones. (must/can't) This girl's mouth and eyes are very different. It _____ be Madonna. (might/might not)

6 It _____ be Jennifer Aniston. Look at her hair. (must/mustn't)

C Complete the sentences with *may/might/could, must* or *can't*.

1 They _____ be South American. They're speaking Spanish.

2 He _____might_____ be American. He's got an Australian accent.

3 Have you carried those suitcases from the station? You _____ be exhausted!

4 It's lunchtime. The shop _____ not be open, but let's go and have a look.

5 This _____ be the right stop. Let's get off the bus here.

6 That shop _____ sell stamps, but I'm not sure.

7 The bill _____ be right. It's too high. The waiter's made a mistake.

8 This hotel _____ have some vacancies. I saw some people checking out just now.

D The police are looking at this tourist's suitcase. Write sentences with *may/might/could, must, can't* or *might not* and a verb.

1 It _____can't be_____ a man. Look at the make-up!

2 She _____ a Japanese speaker. This is a Japanese newspaper.

3 She _____ Japanese. There are a lot of papers in English.

4 She _____ a businesswoman or a film star. Who knows?

5 She _____ a lot of money. That's very expensive jewellery.

6 It _____ someone on holiday. These are business appointments.

30 Unless you hurry

unless (= if not)

	Present	Present/Future (result)
If	I don't wear glasses,	I can't see a thing.
Unless	I wear glasses,	
Unless	you hurry,	you'll be late.

We only use *unless* in real situations, for things that could really happen:

I won't do the cooking	if you don't help me.
	unless you help me.

I'd buy a new car	if I weren't so poor.
	~~unless I were poor.~~

A Which is correct, a or b?

wake up → early → catch train → on time for work → manager pleased → pay rise

wake up → late → miss train → late for work → manager furious → lose job

1 **a** If you wake up early,
    b Unless you wake up early, | you'll miss the train.   ✗ ✓

2 **a** If you catch the train,
    b Unless you catch the train, | you'll be on time for work.

3 **a** If you are on time for work,
    b Unless you are on time, | your manager will be furious with you.

4 **a** If your manager isn't pleased with you,
    b Unless your manager is furious with you, | you'll lose your job.

5 **a** If your manager is pleased with you,
    b Unless your manager is pleased with you, | you won't get a pay rise.

B Complete the sentences.

1 You won't catch the train unless *you wake up early.*

2 You'll catch the train unless _____

3 You'll be late for work unless _____

4 Your manager won't be very pleased with you unless _____

5 You won't lose your job unless _____

6 You'll get a pay rise if _____

7 Unless you want to lose your job, _____

Test 3 (Units 21–30)

A Circle the correct form.

1 It's **very/absolutely** impossible for me to get there earlier.

2 She was **so/such** ill that she couldn't get out of bed.

3 He's a friend of **me/mine**.

4 This sweater is **far more light/far lighter** than the other one.

5 We're thinking **of/in** going out later.

6 I'm sure you**'ll/might** get better soon.

7 She'll come and see you tomorrow if she **has/had** time.

8 After breakfast he **got dressed/got dressed himself** and went to work.

9 Look at all those cigarettes. He **can't/must** smoke a lot.

10 Don't leave unless I**'ll tell/tell** you to.

| 10 |

B Complete the sentences with the correct alternative.

1 It's _____ cold today. (really/completely)

2 There was _____ a long queue at the supermarket. (so/such)

3 After the race the swimmers were _____ exhausted. (totally/awfully)

4 I've got _____ many things to do today. (so/such)

5 She was _____ furious with him for losing the keys. (very/absolutely)

| 5 |

C Write the correct possessive form.

1 That brother of _____ is very annoying. (you)

2 The best rooms are at the _____ . (front/hotel)

3 Is that _____? (your husband/car)

4 She broke _____ leg skiing. (she)

5 I'll meet you at the _____ . (station/railway)

| 5 |

D Complete the sentences with a comparative.

1 His desk is _____ hers. (much/tidy)

2 This house is _____ that one. (not quite/expensive)

3 I'm _____ I was an hour ago. (a bit/hungry)

4 England is _____ France. (not nearly/big)

5 This camera is _____ that camera. (far/cheap)

| 5 |

E Write the correct preposition and the correct form of the verb.

1 They succeeded _____ (climb) to the top of the mountain.
2 We were very worried _____ (get) home late.
3 What are the advantages _____ (buy) a new car?
4 She insisted _____ (do) the work herself.
5 I'm not very good _____ (say) the right thing.

`5`

F Complete the sentences with *'ll/won't, may/might/might not, must* or *can't.*

1 The car _____ be in the station car park, but I'm not sure.
2 I expect we _____ see you tomorrow.
3 That _____ be his son. They're the same age!
4 She knows a lot about plays. She _____ go to the theatre a lot.
5 We want to go away but we _____. It depends on the weather.

`5`

G Write the verbs in the correct form.

1 If I _____ (know) the right answer, I'd tell you.
2 I'll make the reservation unless you _____ (call) me this afternoon.
3 You _____ (play) the piano a lot better if you practised.
4 If there _____ (not/be) any trains tonight, I might get a taxi.
5 Unless you _____ (tell) me the whole story, I won't be able to help you.

`5`

H Complete the sentences with the correct reflexive pronoun or *X* (no pronoun).

1 Last night she went out by _____ .
2 I fell and hurt _____ quite badly.
3 He always shaves _____ before breakfast.
4 Don't worry about them. They can look after _____ .
5 Have you two introduced _____ to the others?

`5`

I Correct the mistakes.

1 It was <u>a such big</u> mistake. _____
2 I look forward <u>to see</u> you later. _____
3 We really <u>enjoyed</u> at the party last night. _____
4 If I <u>would be</u> you, I'd buy a sports car. _____
5 It <u>mustn't</u> be the postman at the door – it's too early. _____

`5`

TOTAL `50`

31 The car's been sold

Passive (*be* + past participle)

	Present continuous	+ past participle	
My watch	is being	repaired.	(Active: Someone is repairing my watch.)
Your shirts	are being	ironed.	

	Present perfect	+ past participle	
This coat	has never been	worn.	(Active: No one has ever worn this coat.)
	Have your keys been	stolen?	

ⓘ We use the passive when we do not know, or it is not important, who does something. The passive often sounds formal.

ⓘ My watch *is being repaired* at the moment. Watches *are* usually *repaired* in two days.
My keys *have been stolen*. It's a disaster! My keys *were stolen* yesterday. It was a disaster.

A What's happening? Complete the sentences with the verbs in the correct form.

1 Sorry you couldn't book on the internet. Our website *'s being redesigned* at the moment. (redesign)

2 You can't check in until 12.00. The rooms _____ . (still/clean)

3 Your bill _____ (prepare) at the moment. Can you come back in a couple of minutes?

4 The drinks machine _____ (still/mend). It'll be OK in an hour or so.

5 You can put your luggage in the meeting rooms. They _____ (not/use) at the moment.

6 Why don't you have something to eat? Breakfast _____ (still/serve) in the dining room.

B What has or hasn't happened? Complete the sentences with a verb from the box in the correct form.

> repair   take   paint   add   (not) wash   (not) lay

1 I think we're too early for dinner. The tables *haven't been laid* yet.

2 The dining room looks lovely. It _____ since we were last here.

3 These sheets _____ . They're still dirty!

4 A big service charge _____ to the bill. I'm going to complain!

5 _____ (the lift)? It was out of order yesterday.

6 What's happened? The television _____ from our room.

49

C Write the verbs in the present continuous or present perfect. Choose the active or passive.

In the past year, three new self-catering apartments (1) _have been built_ (build) with views over the Mediterranean Sea and the Greek Islands. All the rooms (2) _____ (design) with the tourist in mind and at the moment they (3) _____ (decorate) to the highest possible standards. In order to bring all our properties up to the same standard, in the last few months we (4) _____ (modernise) our older apartments near Kaş: air-conditioning (5) _____ (install) and currently all the kitchen equipment (6) _____ (replace).
Looking to the future, we (7) _____ (decide) to develop a new location, and to that end we (8) _____ (purchase) a piece of land with beautiful mountain views on the road east from Kalkan. At the moment no decisions (9) _____ (make) about the best kind of accommodation to put on this site but we are confident that in two years' time excellent accommodation will be available for guests.

D Rewrite the sentences below in the passive to make them more formal.

1 We are improving our services.
   Our services _are being improved._

2 We are equipping the kitchens to the highest possible standard.
   The kitchens _____

3 We have put in washing machines.
   Washing machines _____

4 We are providing extra space for a children's play area.
   Extra space _____

5 We have removed all the rubbish from the site.
   All the rubbish _____

6 We have received no complaints.
   No complaints _____

E Write sentences about recent changes in your town using the present continuous passive or present perfect passive. Think of houses, shops, roads, entertainment, parks and markets.

1 _Many new shops have been built._

2 _____

3 _____

4 _____

5 _____

32 Until I go out

until/before/by the time

Future/Imperative/Request	Present simple
	(Events that happen second)
Wait here	**until** they get back.
Can you close the window	**before** you go out?
She'll be gone	**by the time** he gets home.

PAST   NOW   SECOND EVENT (FUTURE)

          ├───────until───────→ (up to the second event)

         ├───────before─────── (at an earlier time)

           ├──────by the time──────→ (on or before; not later than the second event)

We use *until/before/by the time* when we say that one action happens before another.

ⓘ When we start the sentence with the second event, we use a comma:
Before you go out**,** can you close the window?

A Match the two parts of these voicemail messages.

1 I'll call you again

2 By the time you hear this,

3 I can't take any calls now

4 Before you speak to anyone,

5 Until I see you,

6 The food will be ready

a I'll be on my way to Japan.

b by the time you get here.

c before I leave tonight.

d don't tell anyone the news.

e give me a call.

f until I'm free later in the afternoon.

B Write the verbs in the present simple or the *will* (*'ll*) future.

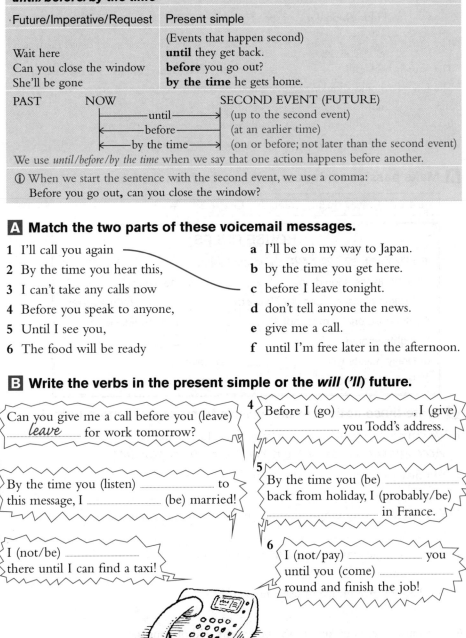

1 Can you give me a call before you (leave) _leave_ for work tomorrow?

2 By the time you (listen) _____ to this message, I _____ (be) married!

3 I (not/be) _____ there until I can find a taxi!

4 Before I (go) _____, I (give) _____ you Todd's address.

5 By the time you (be) _____ back from holiday, I (probably/be) _____ in France.

6 I (not/pay) _____ you until you (come) _____ round and finish the job!

51

33 It'll be done tomorrow

Passive (*be* + past participle)

	Future/Modal +	*be* + past participle
The match	will/won't is (not) going to	be cancelled. (Active: The referee will cancel the match.)
The church	can/can't	be seen for miles. (Active: You can see the church ...)
The job	should/shouldn't	done.
She	must/mustn't	be told.
It	has to/doesn't have to	discussed.
They	may (not)/might (not)	changed.

A Make passive sentences using verbs from the box.

> turn off   leave   bring   replace   give   ask   ~~keep~~

HOUSE RULES

1 Milk must _____*be kept*_____ in the fridge.

2 Dirty dishes should not _____ in the sink.

3 Broken glasses, cups, etc. have to _____ by the guest.

4 Alcoholic drinks must not _____ into the house.

5 Lights should _____ at midnight.

6 Noisy guests will _____ to leave.

7 Refunds cannot _____ under any circumstance.

B Write these notices in the passive to make them more formal.

1 We can arrange your accommodation with local families.
   Accommodation can be arranged with local families.

2 You may park your cars in the car park.

3 You can leave your empty suitcases in the downstairs cupboard.

4 We will charge extra days at a special daily rate.

5 You have to give notice to leave in writing.

6 You must leave your keys in the box at the end of your stay.

C Complete the details with a modal + verb in the passive or active.

SCHOOL OF MUSIC SUMMER INSTITUTE – SCHOLARSHIPS AVAILABLE

This year a small number of scholarships (1) _*are going to be made*_ (going to/make) available for people in low-paid work. However, scholarships (2) _____ (will/only/offer) to candidates with a good musical background. An application form (3) _____ (can/complete) online, but applicants (4) _____ (must/send) us a photograph and a letter of reference by post no later than the end of March. Applications (5) _____ (will/not/consider) after that date. Please note that the School (6) _____ (may/require) applicants to attend an interview but unfortunately travel expenses (7) _____ (can/not/pay). Successful applicants (8) _____ (will/inform) of the School's decision within six weeks of the closing date.

D Write sentences in the passive.

1 This year's Summer Institute/going to/hold/in July
This year's Summer Institute _is going to be held in July._

2 The violinist Maxim Vengerov may/invite to give classes
The violinist Maxim Vengerov _____

3 Lessons will/give in the mornings
Lessons _____

4 Fees/must/pay in advance
Fees _____

5 Students/will/not expect/bring their own instruments
Students _____

6 A welcome party/will/hold on the first night
A welcome party _____

E Complete these predictions with *will* + the passive form of the verb in brackets.

1 When I retire, I hope that I (give) _'ll be given a big present._

2 In 20 years' time, houses (build) _____

3 One day, English (speak) _____

4 Soon, smoking (make) _____

5 In a few years' time, most of the housework (do) _____

34 What does it look like?

look/sound/taste/feel/smell like

What	does	it	look sound taste feel smell	like?	It's	green. noisy. sour. soft. awful!	It	looks like a vegetable. sounds like thunder. tastes like lemon. feels like wool. smells like gas.
Who	does	he	look sound	like?	He looks like his brother. He sounds like his father.			

ⓘ It looks like a vegetable. (*like* = similar to)

ⓘ 'What does Frank look like?' (Describe his appearance.) 'He's very tall.'
'What's Frank like?' (Describe his character/appearance.) 'He's very quiet. And he's tall.'

ⓘ feel like: I feel like a child. (*like* = similar to) I feel like a swim. (= I want to go for a swim.)

A Match the questions with the answers. Then match with the pictures below.

1 What does it look like?   **a** Soft, like leather, but made of plastic. ....

2 What do they taste like?   **b** Like a blanket with a hole for your head. *C*

3 What does it sound like?   **c** Very strong, but delicious to eat! ....

4 What does it feel like?   **d** Quite delicate – a bit like chicken! ....

5 What do they smell like?   **e** Very strange, like someone singing. ....

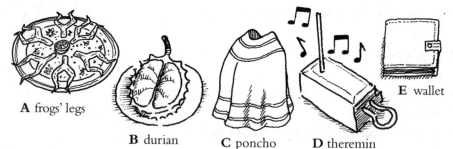

A frogs' legs

B durian

C poncho

D theremin

E wallet

B Complete the gaps with a verb + *like* in the correct form.

1 When Tim speaks, he _sounds like_ a child.

2 The twins .... their mother. They've got the same round eyes.

3 This tea is very weak. It .... water!

4 Every time I go back to my home town I .... a stranger, and I want to leave.

5 What's he cooking? It .... very strong fish. Let's close the window!

6 Everyone was very tired. It was only 8 o'clock, but it .... midnight.

35 Has it been raining?

Present perfect continuous

▶▶ Verb forms page 68

Questions			Short answers		
		been + *-ing* form			
Have	I/you/we/they	been sleeping?	Yes, No,	I/you/we/they	have. haven't.
Has	he/she/it		Yes, No,	he/she/it	has. hasn't.

Questions with question word	
What have you been doing?	(I've been) Working all morning!
How long have you been working?	For four hours./Since 8 o'clock.
Who's been using my computer?	John has.

A Write the verbs in the correct form of the present perfect continuous.

1 'Sorry I'm late. (you/wait) *Have you been waiting* for ages?' 'No, we *haven't* .'

2 'How (your son/get on) _____ at college?' 'Very well.'

3 'You look wet! (you/swim) _____?' 'Yes, I _____ .'

4 '(she/read) _____ my letters?' 'No, she _____!'

5 'How long (your brother/live) _____ in Spain?' 'Two years.'

6 '(you/work) _____ this morning?' 'No, I _____ .'

7 'Who (play) _____ with my mobile phone?' 'Sandra _____ .'

8 'What (you/do) _____?' 'Getting my coat and paying the bill.'

B Write questions for these situations.

1 You see a friend. You haven't seen him for a week. (you/do)
What *have you been doing* _____ recently?

2 You ask about your friend's wife. She's having piano lessons. (she/play)
How long _____ the piano?

3 You meet your son. His eyes are red. (you/cry)
Why _____?

4 Somebody has used your camera. There's no more film in it. (take)
Who _____ photographs with my camera?

5 Tom's father is wearing glasses. You've never seen him in glasses before. (he/wear)
How long _____ glasses?

36 A piece of paper

A **Match the pairs of sentences.**

1 a Can you buy a ———— 1 milk?
  b Can you buy some ———— 2 carton of milk?

2 a I need some   1 olive oil.
  b I need a   2 bottle of olive oil.

3 a Can you get a   1 meat?
  b Can you get some   2 kilo of beef?

4 a Angela wants a   1 rice.
  b Mike wants some   2 packet of rice.

5 a Could I have some   1 cheese?
  b Could I have a   2 piece of cheese?

6 a Get her a   1 honey.
  b Get her some   2 jar of honey.

B **Underline the correct answers. In some cases there is more than one correct answer.**

1 There **wasn't**/**weren't** any sugar.   2 There were **no**/**any** chocolates.

3 They had **some**/**any** tuna.   4 They didn't have **a**/**some**/**any** bread.

5 They didn't have much **chicken**/**chickens**.

6 I didn't buy **much**/**many**/**a lot of** mineral water.

7 They only had **a few**/**a little**/**a couple of** flavours of ice cream.

8 **Much**/**Some**/**Several** of the oranges were bad.

C Look at the ingredients. (✓ = you don't need much/many; ✓✓ = you need a lot.) Complete the sentences with *a/an, a little/a few, a lot of* or *much/many*.

We need (1) ___a little___ butter and olive oil but we need (2) ....
milk and cheese. We don't need (3) .... flour and we don't need
(4) .... eggs. Of course we need (5) .... onion,
(6) .... pasta and (7) .... salt and pepper.

D Complete these sentences from a recipe for tuna pasta bake.
Choose one of the words in brackets and underline the correct noun.

1 Cook the pasta in boiling water for (several, a little) _several_ minute/<u>minutes</u>.

2 Fry the onion in (some, any, much) .... olive oil/olive oils.

3 Heat (a few, a little, many) .... butter/butters in a frying
   pan, add (many, some) .... flour/flours and stir for a
   minute before adding the milk.

4 Add the pasta and the onion, (a few, a lot of, much) ....
   tuna/tunas and cheese/cheeses, and the hard-boiled egg/eggs, and stir for
   (some, much) .... time/times.

5 Add (a few, some, any) .... salt and pepper/salts and
   peppers to taste and heat in an oven for 30 minutes.

6 It's a good idea to serve this dish with (a few, a little, much)
   .... courgette/courgettes or (a, much) ....
   .... small salad/small salads.

E Make a list of what you need for a traditional dish from your country.
Use words like *a, some, a couple of, a little, a lot, plenty of*.

1 *a little flour* ....

2 ....

3 ....

4 ....

5 ....

37 I've been working there

A **Underline the better alternative in these extracts from an article about Placido Domingo.**

1 Placido Domingo is a great opera singer and conductor. Over the years he **has appeared**/has been appearing in all the great opera houses of the world.
2 He **has made**/has been making studio recordings of great operas since 1968 and he's still making them.
3 In the last 33 years he has given/**has been giving** over 600 performances at the Metropolitan Opera in New York.
4 He **has never performed**/has never been performing Wagner's *Tristan and Isolde* on stage, but recently he's worked/**'s been working** on a recording and he hopes to finish it soon.
5 He has sung/**has been singing** for so long he will find it difficult to retire.
6 Apart from music, he **has always loved**/has always been loving motor racing and football.

Placido Domingo
Born in Madrid in 1941

B **Write a journalist's questions to Placido Domingo in the present perfect or present perfect continuous.**

1 you/always/like Verdi? *Have you always liked Verdi?*
2 How many times/you/sing Otello? ....
3 you/conduct/for a long time? ....
4 How many orchestras/you/conduct? ....
5 You're over 60 now. you/work/less recently? ....
6 you/take/the decision to stop singing? ....

C Complete these two letter extracts from Ashok. Write the verbs in the present perfect or present perfect continuous.

Dear Remi
I (1) _____ *have been* _____ (be) back in London for a year now and
I (2) _____ (not/write) to you yet. Sorry! I hope you
(3) _____ (not/wait) for a letter. As you know, I
(4) _____ (take) a course in journalism. I'm still
enjoying it but I (5) _____ (not/have) any free time
recently because of exams and a part-time job. Also, for several weeks
I (6) _____ (try) to find work with a local newspaper.
The good news is that I think I (7) _____ (find) the
perfect job at last!

Dear Sir/Madam
I'm writing in reply to your recent advertisement for a journalist. As you can see from my
CV, for the last year I (8) _____ (study) journalism in London.
The course finishes in June, and we (9) _____ (just/take) our
exams. Unfortunately, we (10) _____ (not/have) the results yet.
Although I (11) _____ (never/work) for a newspaper, I have some
experience of journalism. For the last three months, I (12) _____
(work) as one of the editors on the college magazine, at the same time as I
(13) _____ (revise) for my exams. The experience
(14) _____ (be) exhausting but very enjoyable.

D The interviewers are looking at Ashok's application. Complete the sentences.

1 '(study/he) _____ *Has he studied* _____ journalism?'
  'Yes, he (be) _____ at a college in London for the past year.'

2 '(take/his exams) _____ yet?'
  'Yes, he (just/finish) _____ them.'

3 '(work/he) _____ for a newspaper before?'
  'No, but for the last year he (help) _____ to edit the college
  magazine.'

4 'How long (he/look) _____ for a job?'
  'I don't know. Not long, probably.'

E Complete these sentences about yourself.

1 I've never written _____ .

2 I've sometimes _____ .

3 I've _____ since _____ .

4 I've been _____ ing _____ this year.

5 I haven't _____ this month.

38 He said it was late

A Complete these sentences with the correct pronoun.

1 'I love weddings.' 'Tara said __she__ loved weddings.'
2 'Your mother's crying.' 'She told _____ my mother was crying.'
3 'My name's Raoul.' 'He said _____ name was Raoul.'
4 'You look tired.' 'Jessica told _____ I looked tired.'
5 'I can't see your name on the list.' 'He said _____ couldn't see my name.'

B These are conversations at the wedding party. Write *said* or *told* and the correct form of the verb.

1 I love the music.
Beckie __told__ me she __loved__ the music.
2 My wife's in Scotland.
Brad _____ me his wife _____ in Scotland.
3 Chris will probably be late.
He _____ that Chris _____ probably be late.
4 I don't know why they invited Jack.
She _____ she _____ why they invited Jack.
5 You can have some more to eat.
Mike _____ us that we _____ some more to eat.
6 I have to leave early.
Karen _____ me she _____ leave early.
7 We're staying at the Ritz hotel.
Jacob and Rita _____ they _____ at the Ritz Hotel.

C Complete the sentences from an article about Roger Federer after his victory in the Wimbledon Championships.

1 Winning Wimbledon is an absolute dream for me.
He told me (that) *winning Wimbledon was an absolute dream for him.*

2 I just can't believe it.
He said ....

3 I'm very happy to be part of the history of Wimbledon.
He said .... the history of Wimbledon.

4 I don't know what to say.
He told ....

5 I still miss my first coach, who died in a car accident.
He told ...., who died in a car accident.

6 In my spare time I enjoy deep-sea fishing.
He said .... spare time.

D Complete the replies using the word(s) in brackets.

1 I love tennis. (hate)
But you said *you hated tennis.*

2 The women's final is today. (tomorrow)
But you told me ....

3 Federer will win! (Henman)
But you said ....

4 The match doesn't start until 2.00 pm. (1.00 pm)
But you told me ....

5 I'm sorry there aren't any tickets left for the men's final. (a lot of)
But you said ....

E Read the conversation. Next day Sue tells her friend about it. First, underline the verbs that need to change. Then write what Sue says.

Martin: <u>I'm enjoying</u> the match a lot.
Sue: I'm not. I can't see very well. There are too many people standing in front of me.
Martin: I'll look for some other seats.
Sue: It doesn't matter. I'm going. I have to be back at the office before it closes.

Martin said *he was enjoying the match* a lot but I told ....
because .... very well. There ....
standing in front of me. Martin said .... some other seats.
I told .... because ....
I .... back at the office before ....

39 Do you know everyone?

any/every

We sometimes use *any* in positive sentences to mean 'it's not important which':
Tell me if you have **any** problems.
'Which flavour ice cream would you like?' '**Any** (of them).' (= Any flavour.)

We use *every* to mean 'all':
Every book in the library is very old.

anyone (it doesn't matter who)/*everyone* (all the people):
If **anyone** asks for me, tell them I'm out. **Everyone** makes mistakes.

anything (it's not important what)/*everything* (all the things):
You can do **anything** you want. **Everything** is going well.

anywhere (it's not important where)/*everywhere* (all the places):
I'm really tired. I could sleep **anywhere**. **Everywhere** in Rome is crowded.

ⓘ *any* + plural countable (*any newspaper is* ...) and uncountable nouns (*any time is* ...);
every + singular countable noun (*every house is* ...)

A Underline the correct alternative in these adverts.

1 There are no reservations on our flights. You can have **any**/every seat you like.

2 Any/Every bedroom has its own private bathroom.

3 Our chocolates are more delicious than **any**/every you've eaten in your life before!

4 Any/Every complaints should be addressed to the manager.

5 You'll enjoy **any**/every minute of this wonderful film. Get the DVD now!

6 Don't just buy **any**/every car! Buy a BMW – they're the best.

B Complete these personal adverts with *any/every, anyone/everyone, anything/everything* or *anywhere/everywhere*.

1 Gentleman looking for lady for romantic relationship. *Any* age or nationality.

2 I am prepared to work .... at .... time. But only for good money!

3 I've looked .... for the first Beatles record. If .... has a copy, let me know. I'd like to buy it.

4 I have a luxury apartment for sale. .... over $600,000 will be considered.

5 Are you single like me? .... month I have a meeting in London and .... I know there is married. I love shopping trips and the theatre.

6 They say money isn't ...., but it helps! Does .... know a company that offers small loans at low interest?

7 I pay good prices for .... antique furniture in good condition.

8 I find it difficult to learn English. I've tried .... possible method. Can you help?

Verb	+ object/person	+ (not) to	
Positive			
She asked/told	him	to hurry up.	Hurry up!
Negative			Don't be late!
I asked/told	her	not to be late.	
Verb	+ object/person	+ question word	What's the time?
He asked	me	what the time was. where I worked.	Where do you work?
		+ if/whether	Can you swim?
She wanted to know		if I could swim.	

ⓘ When reporting questions, the verb tense usually moves back:
is → was; work → worked; can → could; will → would

A Match the actual words in A with the sentences in B. Complete the sentences with a verb and use *not* if necessary.

A

1 Call me later.
2 Wait for the others.
3 Please help her.
4 Don't come in tomorrow.
5 Work late tonight, will you?
6 Don't close the window!

B

a I asked him _____ late tonight.
b Igor asked me _____ her.
c I told Dido _____ the window.
d Rita asked Duane _to call_ her later.
e She told me _____ tomorrow.
f She told us _____ for the others.

B Use the words to write sentences.

1 (Please book me a flight.) I/Rachel *I asked/told Rachel to book me a flight.*

2 (Answer my phone, will you?) She/Mark _____

3 (Don't leave the door open!) He/me _____

4 (Sit down, will you?) The manager/Carmen _____

5 (Please wait in reception.) I/him _____

6 (Don't touch my computer, will you?) She/Sue _____

7 (Give her the job!) I/Jacob _____

C Carmen's manager has offered her a new job. She is telling a friend. Complete the sentences. Write the words in the correct order.

1 He asked me if (in the company/was/I/happy) *I was happy in the company.*

2 He wanted to know what (were/my ambitions) ....

3 He asked me if (a manager/to be/would like/I) ....

4 He wanted to know if (at the weekends/could/work/I) ....

5 He asked me who (in my team/would like/I) ....

6 He wanted to know what (in a crisis/do/I/would) ....

7 He asked me how much (the job/I/wanted) ....

8 He wanted to know if (the offer/accept/would/I) ....

D Complete the sentences.

1 (What kind of person are you looking for?)

I asked him *what kind of person he was looking for.*

2 (Does the company offer training?)

I asked him ....

3 (Do you think I can do the job?)

I wanted to know ....

4 (When does the job start?)

I asked him ....

5 (How long are the holidays?)

I wanted to know ....

6 (Where will I work?)

I wanted to know ....

7 (What will my new salary be?)

I asked him ....

8 (Who do I report to?)

I wanted to know ....

Test 4 (Units 31–40)

A Circle the correct alternative.

1 She **is interviewed/is being interviewed** at the moment.

2 I'll stay at college until I **get/will get** a job.

3 Don't worry! All your questions **will answer/will be answered**.

4 He looks **like/as** his brother.

5 I've **been painted/been painting** my room.

6 Get **a few/a little/many** apples from the supermarket, will you?

7 Is he still in the kitchen? He**'s cooked/'s been cooking** all morning.

8 You **said/told** that you were leaving tomorrow.

9 There is a television in nearly **any/every** home in the country.

10 He asked me what **was my name/my name was**.

10

B Write the verbs in the correct passive form.

1 That shirt _____ (already/wash) five times this week!

2 _____ (your car/repair) at the moment?

3 _____ (we/will/give) a pay rise next year?

4 The hotel _____ (should/build) by the end of the year.

5 The streets get very dirty. They _____ (have to/clean) twice a day at the moment.

5

C Write the verbs in the present simple or the '*ll* future.

1 Can you give her your phone number before you _____ (leave).

2 Wait until you _____ (see) what I've bought!

3 I _____ (finish) writing the report before I _____ (go) home.

4 It _____ (be) dark by the time you _____ (get) back.

5 He _____ (stay) here until the last person _____ (leave).

5

D Write the verbs in the present perfect or present perfect continuous.

1 So that's where my book is! I _____ (look) for it all day.

2 You look very tired. What _____ (you/do) this morning?

3 Someone _____ (take) my best CDs! Where are they?

4 I _____ (shop) all morning but I _____ (not/buy) anything yet.

5 How many countries _____ (you/visit) in the last three years?

5

E Write the correct alternative.

1 Can you give me _____ advice? (much/several/a piece of)

2 He's brought _____ luggage with him. (any/a lot of/much)

3 Were there _____ people at the party? (a little/much/many)

4 I just felt _____ rain. (a drop of/a few/any)

5 'How _____ sugar is there?' 'Only _____ .' (many/a few/a little/much)

5

F Complete these sentences in reported speech.

1 'Stand up, children!' She asked _____

2 'I don't like Tom.' He said _____

3 'We can't see a thing!' We said _____

4 'Don't hurry, Tara!' I told _____

5 'How much does it cost?' He wanted to know _____

6 'Are you hungry, Lucy?' I asked _____

7 'What are you doing, Mike?' She asked _____

8 'We're very tired, Kate.' I told _____

9 'We'll finish it later.' They said _____

10 'Do you like coffee, John?' He asked _____

10

G Complete the sentences with *any/every, anyone/everyone, anything/everything* or *anywhere/everywhere*.

1 _____ food would be better than no food at all!

2 I've looked _____ for your letter but I can't find it.

3 If _____ sees Alison, ask her to phone me.

4 I enjoyed _____ minute of the concert.

5 Did you notice _____ unusual about him?

5

H Correct the mistakes.

1 A decision has <u>finally taken</u>. ....

2 'What <u>does it like</u>?' 'It's awful.' ....

3 'How long <u>are you learning</u> English?' ....
'For the last three years.'

4 <u>There are</u> a lot of spaghetti. ....

5 She <u>said me</u> that she was having a shower. ....

5

TOTAL **50**

Verb forms

Present simple

Positive		Negative	
I/You/We/They	speak English.	I/You/We/They	don't (do not) speak Japanese.
He/She	speaks English.	He/She	doesn't (does not) speak Japanese.

Questions			Short answers					
Do	I/you/we/they	speak English?	Yes,	I/we/you/they	do.	No,	I/we/you/they	don't.
Does	he/she			he/she	does.		he/she	doesn't.

Present continuous

Positive		Negative	
I'm (am)		I'm not (am not)	
He/She's (is)	waiting.	He/She isn't (is not)	waiting.
You/We/They're (are)		You/We/They aren't (are not)	

Questions			Short answers					
Am	I	leaving?	Yes,	I	am.	No,	I'm not.
Is	he/she			he/she	is.		he/she isn't.
Are	we/you/they			we/you/they	are.		we/you/they aren't.

Past simple

Positive		Negative		
I/He/She/	walked. (regular)	I/He/She/	didn't	walk.
We/You/They	drove. (irregular)	We/You/They		drive.

Questions			Short answers		
Did	I/he/she/we/you/they	go by bus?	Yes,	I/he/she/we/you/they	did.
			No,		didn't.

Past continuous

Positive			Negative		
I/He/She	was	studying.	I/He/She	wasn't (was not)	studying.
You/We/They	were		You/We/They	weren't (were not)	

Questions			Short answers				
Was	I/he/she	studying?	Yes,	I/he/she	was.	No,	I/he/she wasn't.
Were	we/you/they			we/you/they	were.		we/you/they weren't.

Present perfect

Positive			Negative		
I/You've We/They've (have)		moved.	I/You/ We/They	haven't (have not)	moved.
He/She's (has)			He/She	hasn't (has not)	
Questions			**Short answers**		
Have	I/you/we/they	moved?	Yes,	I/you/we/they have. he/she has.	No,	I/you/we/they haven't. he/she hasn't.
Has	he/she					

Present perfect continuous

Positive			Negative		
I/You've We/They've (have)		been swimming.	I/You/ We/They	haven't (have not)	been waiting.
He/She's (has)			He/She	hasn't (has not)	
Questions			**Short answers**		
Have	I/you/we/they	been swimming?	Yes,	I/you/we/they have. he/she has.	No,	I/you/we/they haven't. he/she hasn't.
Has	he/she					

Countable/Uncountable summary

Words like *some/any* + countable/uncountable noun

	some	*any*	*no*	*much*	*many*	*a lot of/* *plenty of*	*several*	*a couple* *of*	*a little*	*a few*
cup (singular countable)	✗	✗	✗	✗	✗	✗	✗	✗	✗	✗
cups (plural countable)	✓	✓	✓	✗	✓	✓	✓	✓	✗	✓
milk (uncountable)	✓	✓	✓	✓	✗	✓	✗	✗	✓	✗

✓ = We can use this word. ✗ = We can't use this word.

Sentence types with words like *some/any*

some
* for positive statements: There is **some** butter in the fridge.
* offers: Would you like **some** butter?
* requests: Can I have **some** butter?
* questions where we expect the answer 'yes': Is there **some** butter in the fridge?

any
* for negative statements: There isn't **any** butter.
* for questions when we do not know the answer: Are there **any** cups?

much
* for negative sentences: There isn't **much** butter.
* for questions: How **much** butter is there?

many
* for negative sentences: There aren't **many** cups.
* for questions: How **many** cups are there?

a lot of
* for positive sentences: There is **a lot of** butter in the fridge.
* for negative sentences: There aren't **a lot of** cups.
* for questions: Is there **a lot of** butter?

a few
* for positive sentences: There are **a few** cups.
* for questions: Are there **a few** cups?

a little
* for positive sentences: There is **a little** butter.
* for questions: Is there **a little** butter?

Irregular verbs

VERB	PAST SIMPLE	PAST PARTICIPLE
be	was/were	been
beat	beat	beaten
become	became	become
begin	began	begun
bend	bent	bent
bet	bet	bet
bite	bit	bitten
blow	blew	blown
break	broke	broken
bring	brought	brought
build	built	built
burn	burned/burnt	burned/burnt
burst	burst	burst
buy	bought	bought
catch	caught	caught
choose	chose	chosen
come	came	come
cost	cost	cost
cut	cut	cut
deal	dealt	dealt
dig	dug	dug
do	did	done
draw	drew	drawn
dream	dreamed/dreamt	dreamed/dreamt
drink	drank	drunk
drive	drove	driven
eat	ate	eaten
fall	fell	fallen
feed	fed	fed
feel	felt	felt
find	found	found
fly	flew	flown
forget	forgot	forgotten
freeze	froze	frozen
get	got	got

VERB	PAST SIMPLE	PAST PARTICIPLE
give	gave	given
go	went	gone/been
grow	grew	grown
hang	hung/hanged	hung/hanged
have	had	had
hear	heard	heard
hide	hid	hidden
hit	hit	hit
hold	held	held
hurt	hurt	hurt
keep	kept	kept
kneel	kneeled/knelt	kneeled/knelt
know	knew	known
lay	laid	laid
lead	led	led
learn	learned/learnt	learned/learnt
leave	left	left
lend	lent	lent
let	let	let
lie	lay	lain
light	lit	lit
lose	lost	lost
make	made	made
mean	meant	meant
meet	met	met
pay	paid	paid
put	put	put
read	read	read
ride	rode	ridden
ring	rang	rung
rise	rose	risen
run	ran	run
say	said	said
see	saw	seen
sell	sold	sold
send	sent	sent
set up	set up	set up

VERB	PAST SIMPLE	PAST PARTICIPLE
shake	shook	shaken
shine	shone	shone
shoot	shot	shot
show	showed	shown
shrink	shrank	shrunk
shut	shut	shut
sing	sang	sung
sink	sank	sunk
sit	sat	sat
sleep	slept	slept
slide	slid	slid
smell	smelled/smelt	smelled/smelt
speak	spoke	spoken
spell	spelled/spelt	spelled/spelt
spend	spent	spent
spill	spilled/spilt	spilled/spilt
split	split	split
spoil	spoiled/spoilt	spoiled/spoilt
spread	spread	spread
stand	stood	stood
steal	stole	stolen
stick	stuck	stuck
swear	swore	sworn
swell	swelled	swelled/swollen
swim	swam	swum
take	took	taken
teach	taught	taught
tear	tore	torn
tell	told	told
think	thought	thought
throw	threw	thrown
understand	understood	understood
wake	woke	woken
wear	wore	worn
win	won	won
write	wrote	written

Answer key

Unit 1

A 3 isn't either; is 4 does too; doesn't
5 aren't either 6 do too

B 2 g 3 d 4 a 5 e 6 b 7 f

C 3 Neither has he. 4 Neither is she.
5 He hasn't. 6 She doesn't.

D 2 Neither did I./I did! 3 So can I./I
can't! 4 So am I./I'm not! 5 So do I./I
don't! 6 Neither have I./I have!
7 So will I./I won't!

Unit 2

A 2 to arrive 3 staying 4 go 5 to pay
6 taking

B 2 to help 3 continue 4 to lend 5 to give
6 pay 7 asking 8 to build

C Answers will vary.

Unit 3

A 2 sings; usually has 3 like; prefers
4 We sometimes go 5 like 6 read; once
or twice a week we go 7 'm reading;
Do you

B 2 do you go; (EXAMPLES: Never!/I
sometimes go) 3 Do you like; Yes, I do./
No, I don't. 4 Do you sometimes listen
to; Yes, I do./No, I don't. 5 Are you
reading; Yes, I am./No, I'm not.
6 Do you prefer; (I prefer) the cinema/
(I prefer) the theatre.

C 1 'm sitting; relaxing; don't like 2 feel;
'm getting; 'm not training; need; 'm
eating; need 3 'm spending; have; doesn't
matter; 's raining; always play 4 'm
writing; 'm waiting; 's getting; always run;
do; 'm practising

D A 2 B 3 C 4 D 1

E 2 play golf 3 swim; cycle 4 play golf; jog
5 Answers will vary. 6 are getting
fitter/are getting lazier

Unit 4

A 2 in 3 at 4 on 5 in 6 on 7 at 8 X 9 in
10 on 11 at 12 X 13 in 14 at

B 3 In April; on 1(st) May 4 In (the)
summer; in (the) autumn 5 In the last
week of January 6 At 12.00 on 1(st)
December 7 In (the) spring
8 On Tuesday 1(st) September

Unit 5

A 2 can 3 'll be able to 4 have been able to
5 being able to 6 be able to 7 can 8 can

B 2 couldn't/wasn't able to 3 can't
4 be able to 5 managed to/was able to
6 been able to 7 be able to

Unit 6

A 2 Neither 3 either 4 Neither 5 both
6 either; both 7 either; neither

B 2 both 3 Neither 4 either 5 Both
6 neither 7 either 8 Neither 9 either
10 both

C 2 Neither Uncle Harry nor Uncle Bill
got married 3 Granny doesn't like either
Aunt Pat or 4 Both Kate and Max were
5 Ken is either an accountant or 6 Both
Dad and Mum 7 Neither Nick nor
Claudia

Unit 7

A 3 To cash a cheque. 4 To order some
flowers. 5 For a ring. 6 To hire a suit.
7 For some advice!

B 2 employed a chef to prepare 3 phoned a
car rental company to hire 4 went to the
post office to send out 5 drove to the
airport to meet 6 phoned the bank to
check

Unit 8

A 2 Are they? 3 Do they? 4 Was it?
5 Did it? 6 Isn't it? 7 Did he?

B 2 Are they? EXAMPLE: Why's that?
3 Does it? EXAMPLE: Are you sure?
4 Was it? EXAMPLE: That's terrible!
5 Can't they? EXAMPLE: I didn't know that.
6 Did it? EXAMPLE: How amazing!
7 Are they? EXAMPLE: Are you sure?
8 Can they? EXAMPLE: That's interesting.

Unit 9

A 2 fell; was working C Superman and Lois Lane 3 spoke; was having A Madonna and Guy Ritchie 4 kissed; went
E Romeo and Juliet 5 saw; was climbing
B John Lennon and Yoko Ono

B 2 were looking; noticed; was enjoying
3 was sitting; fell; started; worked out
4 was working on; turned into; realised; cooked 5 thought; came to; was singing; needed 6 found; was digging; turned out

C 2 At 3.00 pm my brother was sleeping/ slept in his cabin, while I was sunbathing. (At 3.00 pm, while my brother was sleeping/slept ..., I was sunbathing.)
3 As I stood up, I noticed ... (I noticed ... as I stood up.) 4 While I was waiting/ waited ..., I jumped ... (I jumped ... while I was waiting/waited ...) 5 As I was swimming/swam ..., I saw ... (I saw ... as I was swimming/swam ...)

Unit 10

A 2 have to; mustn't 3 don't have to
4 'll have to 5 must 6 mustn't

B 1 must/'ll have to; must/'ll have to
2 have to; had to 3 don't have to
4 mustn't 5 don't have to; mustn't
6 had to 7 have to 8 don't have to
JOB: flight attendant

Test 1 (Units 1–10)

A 1 Neither did I. 2 smoking 3 are you thinking about? 4 on 5 'll be able to
6 either 7 to do 8 Don't you? 9 were enjoying 10 must

B 1 So 2 either 3 Both 4 either 5 Neither

C 1 to help 2 come 3 spending 4 to go
5 having

D 1 can't 2 hasn't been able to work
3 managed to 4 had to 5 don't have to

E 1 at; in 2 in; on 3 at; on 4 in 5 on; X

F 1 usually comes 2 's she talking 3 don't understand 4 was shaving; heard 5 saw; was talking 6 began; was walking

G 1 Do you? 2 Does she? 3 Didn't you?
4 Weren't you?

H 1 So do I 2 make me get up 3 rarely see
4 tomorrow 5 managed to 6 Neither of my brothers 7 to rest/for a rest 8 Has she? 9 was skiing 10 mustn't

Unit 11

A 2 also 3 since 4 Although 5 What's more

B 2 also 3 too/as well 4 Although/Even though 5 However 6 As/Since

Unit 12

A 2 park; No, (you) can't 3 phone/call; no, (you) can't 4 pay; Yes, (you) can 5 can
6 can't

B 2 lending me a pen 3 shut the door
4 wait a minute 5 looking after the children 6 bring me the bill

Unit 13

A 2 has always had 3 appeared; was; has been 4 appeared 5 made 6 have always been; spent

B 1 was; I appeared 2 Have you ever won; have; did you play; was 3 Did you accept; didn't; didn't want; persuaded 4 Have you ever been; did you last go; went
5 Have you ever felt; have always been

C 2 Tara's just given up her job. Apparently, she didn't like (her boss). 3 I've just found my wallet. It was in (my old jacket).
4 Sam's had an accident. His car hit (a tree). 5 We've missed the match. It started (at 5.00).

D 1 was; have always admired; 've known; looked; dressed; was; left; started; has always given 2 first saw; told; got on; has changed; has become; have now reached; moved; saw; met

Unit 14

A 2 where you usually stay 3 when your last visit was 4 how long you are staying this time 5 how you got here 6 which areas you have visited 7 what improvements you would like to see

B All answers begin with one of these: *Do you know ...? Can/Could I ask you ...? Can/Could you tell me ...? Would you mind telling me ...?*
2 ... what time the bank closes?
3 ... which floor the café is on?
4 ... where I can leave my bags?
5 ... when the train leaves?
6 ... how much the ticket costs?

Unit 15

A 1 under 2 against 3 by 4 on; below 5 above 6 inside

B 2 in 3 on 4 at 5 in 6 at 7 in 8 in 9 in 10 by

Unit 16

A 2 will 3 will 4 's going to 5 won't 6 will 7 's going to 8 will never

B 2 The plane for Sweden leaves at 6.30 am.
3 It gets in to Arlanda airport at 10.10.
4 We're having lunch at the Sturehof.
5 We're meeting her manager after lunch.
6 We're going to the Södra theatre in the evening.
7 The play starts at 7.30.
8 It finishes at about 11.00.

Unit 17

A 2 this bus goes to Terminal 1 3 the shops will be open 4 it is very expensive 5 there is a train to the city centre 6 anyone left a message for me 7 the flight has been delayed

B 2 if/whether you buy it directly from Sony 3 if/whether you have ordered from them before 4 if/whether they are working with any other company like yours 5 if/whether you will order from them next year 6 if/whether you came to our annual conference 7 if/whether you are going to continue with the research

Unit 18

A 2 (that/which) a 3 which b 4 (that/which) f 5 who c 6 (who) d

B 2 who/that does medical operations 3 (that/which) we tie round an injury 4 that/which measures our temperature 5 (that/which) we take to cure infection 6 (who/that) we see when we've got toothache

C 2 the doctor who/that looked after me 3 antibiotics (that/which) she gave me were very strong 4 hospital (that/which) I went to is near where I live 5 had an operation that/which was a great success 6 nurses who/that looked after me were great

Unit 19

A 2 moved to the country so (that) their children would have a better way of life 3 sold their flat in the city so (that) they would have enough money to buy a farm 4 lived near a small village so (that) they could get to know people more easily 5 grew their own vegetables so (that) they wouldn't have to buy them

B 2 so expensive (that) 3 so small (that) 4 so poor (that) 5 so hard (that) 6 so happy (that)

Unit 20

A 1 boring 2 depressing; fascinating; amazing 3 horrified; amusing 4 amazed; interesting 5 irritated; fascinated

B 2 exciting 3 bored 4 amazing 5 satisfying 6 irritated 7 fascinating 8 confused 9 disappointing 10 interesting

C Answers will vary. 2 confusing 3 frightened 4 shocked 5 worrying

Test 2 (Units 11–20)

A 1 Although 2 can't 3 went 4 you live 5 under 6 'm staying 7 she is 8 which 9 so dark that 10 fascinating

B 1 However 2 As 3 too 4 even though 5 also

C 1 you want to leave tomorrow 2 answering the phone 3 use your computer 4 the time is 5 he likes French food

D 1 in 2 against 3 at 4 on 5 outside

E 1 Have you been 2 's going to cry
3 've just heard 4 leaves 5 did you arrive

F 1 is the woman who/that lives next door
2 the man (who/that) I was telling you
about 3 bought a coat (that/which) he
didn't really like 4 (that/which) I stayed
in had a swimming pool 5 who/that
spoke English showed us the way

G 1 (that) he could get 2 to get 3 hungry
(that) I ate 4 I ate 5 (that) they could learn

H 1 confused 2 frightening 3 annoying
4 worried 5 exhausting

I 1 pay 2 saw 3 what time the plane leaves
4 (who) I met 5 so

Unit 21
A 2 furious 3 freezing 4 impossible
5 brilliant

B 2 very/awfully/terribly/incredibly/really
cold 3 really/absolutely furious 4 It was
really/absolutely/completely/totally
impossible 5 really/absolutely freezing;
very/awfully/terribly/incredibly/really
tired 6 very/awfully/terribly/incredibly/
really good

C Answers will vary.

Unit 22
A 2 The culture is so varied. 3 We've eaten
such wonderful food. 4 We had such a
lovely day. 5 Our holiday has gone so
quickly.

B 2 such 3 so 4 so 5 such

C 2 The city is so big (that) we soon got
tired. 3 We were so hungry (that) we
stopped at the Hsing Yeh restaurant for a
meal. 4 They were such large dishes
(that) we couldn't eat everything. 5 The
meal was so lovely (that) we left a big tip.

Unit 23
A 2 Andrea's guitar 3 my; mine 4 ours
5 Tom's parents' 6 my violin case
7 women's 8 tomorrow's concert 9 his
10 the name of the song

B 2 Sir Simon Rattle's recording;
Beethoven's opera 3 The name of the
mezzo-soprano, Cecilia Bartoli
4 Alexandre's guitar 5 The results of this
year's competition; the end of the concert

Unit 24
A 3 Bill isn't as heavy as Eddie. 4 Bill is as
light as Frank. 5 Frank is almost as old as
Eddie. 6 Bill isn't nearly as young as
Frank. 7 Eddie is much shorter than Bill.
8 Frank is a bit taller than Eddie.

B 2 quite as good-looking as 3 far more
suntanned than 4 nearly as thin as 5 a lot
bigger 6 a little taller

Unit 25
A 2 in improving 3 at skiing 4 on buying
5 of wearing 6 of flying

B 2 on developing 3 for attracting
4 at creating 5 in selling 6 of upsetting
7 about using 8 to hearing

Unit 26
A 2 will 3 might 4 will 5 will definitely
6 won't 7 will probably 8 probably
won't; will

B 2 Sea levels will definitely rise. 3 Farmers
probably won't be able to plant their
crops near the sea. 4 I don't think some
small islands will survive. 5 The world's
weather will definitely get more extreme.
6 I expect some parts of the world will
get drier. 7 Other parts of the world
might get colder. 8 Unfortunately, I
doubt if we'll ever learn to look after our
environment.

C Answers will vary.

D Answers will vary.

Unit 27
A 2 d 3 f 4 e 5 a 6 c

B 2 were; I'd 3 want; mustn't 4 might feel;
were 5 increased; would 6 'll offer; think
7 can; are 8 get; I'll buy

C Answers will vary.

2 If I have … I'll/If I had … I'd …
3 If I live … I'll/If I lived … I'd …
4 If I decide … I'll/If I decided … I'd …
5 If my computer is stolen … I'll/If my
computer was stolen … I'd …
6 If I wake up … I'll/If I woke up …
I'd …

D 2 If I were you, I'd put on a coat. 3 If I
were you, I'd go by boat. 4 If I were you,
I'd buy a new one. 5 If I were you, I'd
learn Chinese before you go.

E Answers will vary.
2 If I heard someone … I would/might …
3 If an attractive, wealthy person wanted
… I would/might … 4 If I met the US
President … I would/might … 5 If I
spoke English fluently … I would/might …

Unit 28

A 2 yourselves 3 relax 4 himself 5 himself
6 change 7 enjoying yourself 8 myself
9 feel 10 met

B 2 ourselves 3 himself 4 yourselves
5 yourself 6 myself 7 itself 8 yourself

C 2 by herself 3 by itself 4 by myself
5 by themselves

D 2 teaching himself 3 behave themselves
4 buy ourselves 5 look after himself
6 ask myself 7 watching herself
8 tell (me) about yourself

Unit 29

A 2 She can't be … a; She might be … b
3 That can't be … b; That might be … a
4 That must be … a; That might not be … b

B 1 (Britney Spears) 2 might (David
Beckham) 3 must (Leonardo DiCaprio)
4 might (Brad Pitt) 5 can't; might
(Madonna) 6 must (Jennifer Aniston)

C 2 can't 3 must 4 may/might 5 must
6 may/might/could 7 can't 8 must
(may/might/could)

D 2 must be 3 might not be 4 may/might/
could be 5 must have/must earn
6 can't be

Unit 30

A 2 a ✓ b ✗ 3 a ✗ b ✓ 4 a ✓ b ✗
5 a ✗ b ✓

B 2 you wake up late 3 you catch the train
4 you're on time for work 5 you're late
for work 6 your manager is pleased with
you 7 EXAMPLES: don't be late for
work/you mustn't be late for work

Test 3 (Units 21–30)

A 1 absolutely 2 so 3 mine 4 far lighter
5 of 6 'll 7 has 8 got dressed 9 must
10 tell

B 1 really 2 such 3 totally 4 so 5 absolutely

C 1 yours 2 front of the hotel 3 your
husband's car 4 her 5 railway station

D 1 much tidier than 2 not quite as
expensive as 3 a bit hungrier than
4 not nearly as big as 5 far cheaper than

E 1 in climbing 2 about getting 3 of buying
4 on doing 5 at saying

F 1 might/may 2 'll 3 can't (won't) 4 must
5 might not

G 1 knew 2 call 3 'd (would) play 4 aren't
5 tell

H 1 herself 2 myself 3 X 4 themselves
5 yourselves

I such a big 2 to seeing 3 enjoyed ourselves
4 were 5 can't/won't

Unit 31

A 2 are still being cleaned 3 's (is) being
prepared 4 's (is) still being mended
5 're (are) not being used 6 's (is) still
being served

B 2 's (has) been painted 3 haven't been
washed 4 has been added 5 Has the lift
been repaired 6 's (has) been taken

C 2 have been designed 3 are being
decorated 4 have modernised
5 has been installed 6 is being replaced
7 have decided 8 have purchased
9 have been made

D 2 are being equipped to the highest possible standard 3 have been put in 4 is being provided for a children's play area 5 has been removed from the site 6 have been received

E Answers will vary.

Unit 32
A 2 a 3 f 4 e 5 d 6 b

B 2 listen; 'll be 3 won't be 4 go; 'll give 5 're; 'll probably be 6 won't pay; come

Unit 33
A 2 be left 3 be replaced 4 be brought 5 be turned off 6 be asked 7 be given

B 2 Cars may be parked in the car park. 3 Empty suitcases can be left in the downstairs cupboard. 4 Extra days will be charged at a special daily rate. 5 Notice to leave has to be given in writing. 6 Keys must be left in the box at the end of the/your stay.

C 2 will only be offered 3 can be completed 4 must send 5 will not be considered 6 may require 7 cannot be paid 8 will be informed

D 2 may be invited to give classes 3 will be given in the mornings 4 must be paid in advance 5 will not be expected to bring their own instruments 6 will be held on the first night

E Answers will vary. EXAMPLES: 2 will be built (on the moon) 3 will be spoken (everywhere) 4 will be made (illegal) 5 will be done (by robots)

Unit 34
A 2 d A 3 e D 4 a E 5 c B

B 2 look like 3 tastes like 4 feel like 5 smells like 6 felt like

Unit 35
A 2 's (has) your son been getting on 3 Have you been swimming; have 4 Has she been reading; hasn't 5 has your brother been living 6 Have you been working; haven't

7 's (has) been playing; has 8 have you been doing

B 2 has she been playing 3 have you been crying 4 's (has) been taking 5 has he been wearing

Unit 36
A 2 a 1; b 2 3 a 2; b 1 4 a 2; b 1 5 a 1; b 2 6 a 2; b 1

B 2 no 3 chicken 4 some 5 any 6 much/a lot of 7 a few/a couple of 8 Some/Several

C 2 a lot of 3 much/a lot of 4 many/a lot of 5 an 6 a lot of 7 a little

D 2 some olive oil 3 a little butter; some flour 4 a lot of tuna; cheese; eggs; some time 5 some salt and pepper 6 a few courgetttes; a small salad

E Answers will vary.

Unit 37
A 2 has been making 3 has given 4 has never performed; 's (has) been working 5 has been singing 6 has always loved

B 2 How many times have you sung Otello? 3 Have you been conducting (Have you conducted) for a long time? 4 How many orchestras have you conducted? 5 Have you been working less (Have you worked less) recently? 6 Have you taken the decision to stop singing?

C 2 haven't written 3 haven't been waiting 4 have been taking (have taken) 5 haven't had 6 have been trying (have tried) 7 've found 8 have been studying (have studied) 9 have just taken 10 haven't had 11 have never worked 12 have been working/have worked 13 have been revising 14 has been

D 1 has been 2 Has he taken; 's (has) just finished 3 Has he worked; 's (has) been helping/'s (has) helped 4 has he been looking (has he looked)

E Answers will vary.

Unit 38

A 2 me 3 his 4 me 5 he

B 2 told; was 3 said; would 4 said; didn't
know 5 told; could have 6 told; had to
7 said; were staying

C 2 (that) he just couldn't believe it
3 (that) he was very happy to be part of
4 me (that) he didn't know what to say
5 me (that) he still missed his first coach
6 (that) he enjoyed deep-sea fishing in his

D 2 (that) the women's final was tomorrow
3 (that) Henman would win
4 (that) the match started at 1.00 pm
5 (that) there were a lot of tickets left for
the men's final

E Verbs: I'm not; I can't see; There are; I'll
look; It doesn't matter; I'm going; I have
to; it closes
him (that) I wasn't; I couldn't see; were
too many people; (that) he would look
for; him (that) it didn't matter; I was
going; had to be; it closed

Unit 39

A 2 Every 3 any 4 Any 5 every 6 any

B 2 anywhere; any 3 everywhere; anyone
4 Anything 5 Every; everyone
6 everything; anyone 7 any 8 every

Unit 40

A 2 f to wait 3 b to help 4 e not to come
in 5 a to work 6 c not to close

B 2 She asked/told Mark to answer her
phone. 3 He asked/told me not to leave
the door open. 4 The manager
asked/told Carmen to sit down.
5 I asked/told him to wait in reception.
6 She asked/told Sue not to touch her
computer. 7 I asked/told Jacob to give
her the job.

C 2 my ambitions were 3 I would like to
be a manager 4 I could work at the
weekends 5 I would like in my team
6 I would do in a crisis 7 I wanted the
job 8 I would accept the offer

D 2 if/whether the company offered
training 3 if/whether he thought I could
do the job 4 when the job started 5 how
long the holidays were 6 where I would
work 7 what my new salary would be
8 who I reported to

Test 4 (Units 31–40)

A 1 is being interviewed 2 get 3 will be
answered 4 like 5 been painting
6 a few 7 's been cooking 8 said
9 every 10 my name was

B 1 has already been washed 2 Is your car
being repaired 3 Will we be given
4 should be built 5 have to be cleaned
(are having to be cleaned)

C 1 leave 2 see 3 'll finish; go 4 'll be; get
5 'll stay; leaves

D 1 've been looking (have looked)
2 have you been doing (have you done)
3 's (has) taken
4 've been shopping; haven't bought
5 have you visited

E 1 a piece of 2 a lot of 3 many 4 a drop of
5 much; a little

F 1 the children to stand up 2 (that) he
didn't like Tom 3 (that) we couldn't see a
thing 4 Tara not to hurry 5 how much it
cost 6 Lucy if/whether she was hungry
7 Mike what he was doing 8 Kate (that)
we were very tired 9 (that) they would
finish it later 10 John if/whether he liked
(likes) coffee

G 1 Any 2 everywhere 3 anyone 4 every
5 anything

H 1 has finally been taken 2 's (is) it like
3 have you been learning (have you learnt)
4 There is 5 told me/said to me

Acknowledgements

I would particularly like to thank Alison Sharpe for her help, guidance and support during the editing of this series. My thanks also to Tony Garside and Jamie Smith for their expert editing of the material and to Kamae Design and Nick Schon for their excellent design and artwork.

The publisher would like to thank the following for permission to reproduce photographs.

p. 5 Corbis/P. Giardino (man), p. 5 Corbis/R. Lewine (woman), p. 12 Corbis/ J. Klee, p. 15 Corbis/Bettmann (John and Yoko), p. 20 Corbis/D. Congor, p. 25 Corbis/R. Klune, p. 34 Corbis/J. Fuste Raga, p. 50 Corbis/D. G. Houser, p. 56 Corbis/M. S. Yamashita, p. 58 Corbis/Reuters; p. 38 Getty Images/Time Life Pictures; p. 15 The Moviestore Collection (Superman II 1980 Christopher Reeve and Margot Kidder), (Romeo and Juliet 1968 Franco Zefferelli Olivia Hussey and Leonard Whiting), p. 44 The Moviestore Collection (Britney Spears), (Leonardo DiCaprio), (Brad Pitt), (Madonna), (Jennifer Aniston); p. 15 Rex Features/MBP (Madonna and Guy Ritchie), Rex Features/IJO (David and Victoria Beckham). Rex Features, p.22 Rex Features/YPP, p.44 Rex Features/NWI (David Beckham).

Every effort has been made to reach the copyright holders; the publishers would be pleased to hear from anyone whose rights they have unknowingly infringed.

Produced by Kamae Design, Oxford.